The Soft September Air

A Play

Charlotte Hastings

A Samuel French Acting Edition

FOUNDED 1830

SAMUELFRENCH-LONDON.CO.UK
SAMUELFRENCH.COM

Copyright © 1979 by Charlotte Hastings
All Rights Reserved

THE SOFT SEPTEMBER AIR is fully protected under the copyright laws of the British Commonwealth, including Canada, the United States of America, and all other countries of the Copyright Union. All rights, including professional and amateur stage productions, recitation, lecturing, public reading, motion picture, radio broadcasting, television and the rights of translation into foreign languages are strictly reserved.

ISBN 978-0-573-11423-6

www.samuelfrench-london.co.uk

www.samuelfrench.com

FOR AMATEUR PRODUCTION ENQUIRIES

UNITED KINGDOM AND WORLD EXCLUDING NORTH AMERICA

plays@SamuelFrench-London.co.uk

020 7255 4302/01

Each title is subject to availability from Samuel French,

depending upon country of performance.

CAUTION: Professional and amateur producers are hereby warned that *THE SOFT SEPTEMBER AIR* is subject to a licensing fee. Publication of this play does not imply availability for performance. Both amateurs and professionals considering a production are strongly advised to apply to the appropriate agent before starting rehearsals, advertising, or booking a theatre. A licensing fee must be paid whether the title is presented for charity or gain and whether or not admission is charged.

The professional rights in this play are controlled by Samuel French Ltd, 52 Fitzroy Street, London, W1T 5JR.

No one shall make any changes in this title for the purpose of production. No part of this book may be reproduced, stored in a retrieval system, or transmitted in any form, by any means, now known or yet to be invented, including mechanical, electronic, photocopying, recording, videotaping, or otherwise, without the prior written permission of the publisher. No one shall upload this title, or part of this title, to any social media websites.

The right of Charlotte Hastings to be identified as author of this work has been asserted by her in accordance with Section 77 of the Copyright, Designs and Patents Act 1988

THE SOFT SEPTEMBER AIR

CHARACTERS

Lindsey Ashe, a novelist
Mrs Bevil, her daily help
Dickon ⎫
Chris ⎬ University students
Gavin ("Blitz") ⎭
Horace Bellamy, Dickon's father
Di, "Blitz's" liberated girl-friend
First Old Lady
Second Old Lady
Nurse Kelly
Dr Grieves, a lady doctor
Sister
Another Student

The parts of the two Old Ladies can be doubled with Nurse Kelly and Sister. "Blitz" can be doubled with the Student who appears at the end of the play.

The action takes place in Linnets Cottage, at Westfield Green, a village on the outskirts of a university town, and covers a period of twelve months.

Act I September to December
Act II June to September

Time—the present

The songs *The Soft September Air* and *Then and Now* composed by Michael Blanchard

The play was originally broadcast on BBC Radio in October 1978, with the following cast of characters:

Lindsey Ashe	Flora Robson
Dickon Bellamy	Andrew Branch
Mrs Bevil	Betty Hardy
Horace Bellamy	Hector Ross
Gavin (Blitz)	Kenneth Shanley
Chris	Sean Barrett
Millicent/1st Old Girl	Margot Boyd
Phillip/Sergeant	Gavin Campbell
Dr Porteus	Kenneth Barrow
Di	Susan Sloman
Inspector/TV Voice 1	Malcolm Gerrard
Doctor/TV Voice 2	Henry Knowles
Sister/2nd Old Girl	Brenda Kaye
Student/Waiter	Max Hafler
Guitarist	Eric Hill

The play directed by Graham Gauld
Songs composed by Michael Blanchard

Foreword by Dame Flora Robson, who took the part of Lindsey in the radio broadcast of this play.

I have been a great admirer of Charlotte Hastings' work since she wrote a beautiful play—*Bonaventure*. It was a great first night success with Irene Vanburgh, Fay Compton and Mary Kerridge.

When I was given a BBC choice of plays, in a series, I chose *Bonaventure*, since when I have been most happy to follow in a run of her plays on BBC Radio.

I am proud to say we are happy partners with the BBC accepting our choice of stories. Our interests are the same and we both feel we have much to give and receive.

This play, *The Soft September Air*, has splendid parts for mature actresses and some first class young people with their university and personal problems. It presents many interests and incidents common to both of us and I feel it will come to life before an audience.

Flora Robson

To Roger, Duncan, Gerald, Colin, Neil and Michael—
and any others who may follow.

PRODUCTION NOTES

This acting edition of *The Soft September Air* offers societies something a little different from the standard three-acter, with interesting ideas for insets, recordings, etc.

The few costume changes, clearing of hand props, re-setting, lighting etc, have been worked out for a minimum of waiting between scenes. With organization, the play may be almost continuous.

The two inset scenes in the pub and the hospital may be produced in two ways. The simplest—as indicated in the script—is to play them before the CURTAIN. Societies who have no room for this, can lower the CURTAIN after the major scene, set two or three black screens across the stage a few feet from the front, then raise the CURTAIN and play the inset against the screens. At the end of the inset scene, the CURTAIN is lowered while the screens are removed, then raised again on the major scene in the cottage.

Recordings. It is very effective to have the various letters, telephone calls, TV news and the scene in the car recorded and relayed from the side of the stage or the back of the audience. If Dickon cannot play the guitar, the songs may be recorded and played from the wings and he can mime.

If recordings are not possible, the alternatives are simple, as follows:
1. Lindsey reads aloud all the letters from her sister and her literary agent, and her own replies, also the last letter from Dickon at the end of the play.
2. The television news may be read from the wings.
3. The scene in the car may be omitted—but it should be noted this may cut the time allowed for Dickon to change into his dark suit for the next act.
3. The interlude of the song in the pub ('Then and Now') and the audience participation may be omitted. In which case it is suggested that when Lindsey and Chris exit to go into the lounge, a burst of music and laughter etc., is heard behind the CURTAIN, and the two old ladies also exit into the wings.
4. The telephone conversations with Dr Porteus may be simplified into the dialogue, as follows:

Page 25

Lindsey Westfield three-seven .... Who? ... Dr Porteus, oh, yes, the Dean of Students, isn't it? Good evening ... Gavin Marsh? Yes, but he isn't here at the moment ... Oh no! Don't say he's come off that wretched bike? ... No? Then what ... Back here tomorrow, yes, I see ... (*Slowly*) He's not in hospital? ... Well, no—not just for a few bruises, but what has ... You're looking after him? I—see. Thank you, Dr Porteus—it is very kind of you to let me know ... Yes—good-bye.

Page 45 (*played before the* CURTAIN)

Chris Westfield three-seven... No, Mrs Ashe is out... Oh, Dr Porteus, Chris here. Chris Conway. Is it about Dickon? I've been out looking for the last two hours. Is he on campus?... Westfield General?... I knew he'd come off that bike... What!... An overdose! (*Quietly*) Oh, my God—he's not... I see. Where did they find him?... Yes... No, there wouldn't be an answer—his father's down here—at the Royal. And Mrs Ashe. Just a moment, are you at the hospital?... Right, I'll get out to the Royal and bring them over. Where do we go—Casualty?... Reception... The Park Street entrance—I know. I'm on my way. (*He mimes replacing the phone and hurries out through the* CURTAIN)

ACT I

Scene 1

The living-room of Linnets Cottage, Westfield Green, a village on the outskirts of a university town. Afternoon

The room is a period one, of some taste and elegance, with beamed walls and ceiling. A brick fireplace with hood is in the middle of the back wall, with a wide, practical sash window and window seat to one side. The curtains and seat cushions are in chintz. To the other side of the fireplace are crowded bookshelves: on the middle shelf are a sherry decanter, brandy, and various glasses. In the wall below the sash window is the main door leading to the hall and the rest of the cottage: between this door and the window is a corner cupboard with an attractive green dessert service. Opposite the door is another large window. A big desk stands at this window, with a swivel chair before it, back to the door. On the desk are various papers, writing materials, etc., a telephone and a typewriter. Between the desk and the bookshelves is a small table with an electric kettle, coffee and mugs. There is also a comfortable settee

When the CURTAIN *rises the room is empty. Lindsey Ashe enters from the hall, carrying a gardening basket. She puts it on the window seat and crosses to the desk, pulling off her gardening gloves. She is a handsome, intelligent woman of fifty-eight wearing country clothes. A moment later Mrs Bevil follows her in, a stocky countrywoman of about sixty-five. She wears a tweed skirt, light sweater and "coverall" apron*

Mrs Bevil —and there's no need to go on your knees to them weeds. Bevil'll be up Saturday.

Lindsey I wanted to finish that border. Saturday we'll lift the dahlias. (*She sits at the desk and turns over some manuscripts*)

Mrs Bevil We don't never lift ours. Bevil don't hold with it. (*She moves to the desk*) Your supper's in the oven and there's a mousse in the fridge. You said you fancied chocolate, but I think the lemon's nicer.

Lindsey (*absently*) Thank you, Bev.

Mrs Bevil And George Billings just brought up late post. (*She takes three letters from apron pocket—one in a blue envelope*) Two bills—one's the 'lectric—(*she gives them to Lindsey*)—and this one I reckon'll be from your sister.

Lindsey Oh dear—so it is. How tiresome.

Mrs Bevil (*grimly*) Ah. She'll not be best pleased when she knows what you're up to. And I'll get gone myself—before this long-haired layabout arrives.

Lindsey Bev—students are not all long-haired layabouts . . .

Mrs Bevil Worst thing they ever did—putting that university in the town. All them up there—living off social security—
Lindsey —and student grants are not social security.
Mrs Bevil I don't know why we bother to vote. Bevil says what we want now is a collision Government.
Lindsey Oh, *Bev* . . .
Mrs Bevil And we certainly don't want one of that lot up here—disturbing all the peace and quiet.
Lindsey I cannot be alone at night in this isolated house any longer. And one boy studying quietly in his room, is not going to disturb *anything*.
Mrs Bevil Thass as maybe. (*She takes the gloves and goes to the window seat for the basket*) See you in the morning.

Mrs Bevil goes out with the basket

Lindsey (*calling*) Thank you, Bev. (*Looking at the blue envelope*) Oh dear, if I read this now it will spoil my appetite and if I read it later it will give me indigestion. I think—yes, I'll read it now and then have a very large sherry. (*She opens the letter*) And one thing's for sure, Lindsey my girl. If there's to be someone else in the house you'll have to stop talking to yourself. Now—where're my glasses. (*She finds them on the desk and either reads the letter aloud, or Millicent's recorded voice is heard, high, precise and rather censorious. See Production Note*) My dear Lindsey: This idea of taking an irresponsible student into your house is preposterous. You cannot need the money. Your writing does very well, though we have never been able to understand why. However we do appreciate your fear of being alone in Linnets at night after that attempted break-in, and Cedric wishes me to say we are prepared—(*she turns*) *the page*)

A motor-cycle is heard arriving

—to make a home for you with us. We cannot offer you separate accommodation, but there are two good rooms upstairs with quite a pleasant view over the kitchen garden, and Cedric has generously offered to put in a gas ring. Isn't this hot weather *trying*. Your affectionate sister, Millicent. P. S. It's a pity you are not more domesticated. You never did know one end of a dishcloth from another.
Lindsey (*angrily*) Oh, hell and damnation . . . !
Dickon (*calling, off*) Hullo!

Dickon appears at the casement window. He is nearly twenty-one, tall and good looking with a very pleasant speaking voice. His hair is worn just below his ears, but well-groomed. He wears jeans and a crash helmet

Dickon I'm from the university . . .
Lindsey I'm sorry, I didn't hear . . . (*She rises and crosses to the window*)
Dickon The Housing Office sent me. (*Suddenly*) My God . . .
Lindsey What *is* the matter?
Dickon This house. I've never seen anything quite so beautiful. The thatch—and the walls—with that kind of scroll pattern . . .

Act I Scene 1

Lindsey Pargetting.
Dickon Par . . . ?
Lindsey Pargetting. Made with a pointed stick while the plaster is still wet. One of the medieval building crafts.
Dickon How old is it?
Lindsey So far as we've been able to ascertain—(*she sits on the window seat, resting one hand on the sill*)—it's fifteenth century.
Dickon I can't wait to come here. Please—*dear* lady—take me in. Look—on my knees—"I do entreat thee—in compassion's name . . ."
Lindsey (*laughing*) Don't be an idiot. Get up. No—I don't want my hand kissed. Get up and give me a few details.

He gets up and takes off his helmet

Dickon Bellamy, Richard Paul. Known as Dickon. Twenty-one in six weeks' time. Third year—reading English Lit. Honest, sober and reasonably industrious. Only vice—playing the guitar. I think you are as beautiful as your house—and please may I now kiss your hand?
Lindsey Lindsey Ashe. Novelist. Widowed five years. As I desire above all things to remain in this cottage I need someone in the house at night because . . .
Dickon I will defend you both to the death and beyond. (*Getting up*) May I move in now?
Lindsey I have not yet said you may move in at all.
Dickon Then I will hang myself from one of those willows and you may gaze from your window at my dangling, twitching body . . .
Lindsey (*interestedly*) What with?
Dickon Sorry?
Lindsey With what will you hang yourself? There must be something to support your dangling twitching body?
Dickon Oh. Do you—do you have a clothes-line?
Lindsey (*gravely*) We could not spare it. It is in constant use.
Dickon I—see. No other piece of rope available? Thick string? Or garden twine?
Lindsey Regretfully, no. This is a thrifty house.
Dickon Then I will drown myself in that beautiful pond—"There is a willow grows aslant a brook . . ."
Lindsey (*abruptly*) It is only two feet deep.
Dickon So you condemn me to live.
Lindsey It would appear so.
Dickon But to condemn me to live miserably—is that not illogical?
Lindsey Not in the least. Why don't you want to live at the University?
Dickon On campus? You must be joking. I've stuck it for two years—two years of hell. Please let me come here. (*His tone changes completely. Quietly*) I think—I think I might find peace in this place.

Lindsey gets up. They look at each other for a second

Lindsey (*also quietly*) The front door is at the side. Just—lift the latch and come in.

A sports car roars up and stops

Chris (*calling, off*) I say—! Is this Linnets?

A car door slams. Steps are heard.

>*Chris appears in the window. He is about the same age as Dickon, stocky, sensible and very practical; wears the inevitable uniform of sweater and jeans*

I'm from the University. The Housing Office said . . .
Lindsey I'm afraid you're just too late. Oh—this is Dickon Bellamy.
Chris Chris Conway. Hi.
Dickon Hi.
Chris What a marvellous place. Couldn't you possibly fit me in somewhere?
Dickon I shouldn't think that old banger would bring you. Where on earth did you salvage it?
Chris You leave her alone—the only woman in my life at the moment. Look—wouldn't a house like this have more than two bedrooms?
Lindsey Two double rooms and a bit of an attic.
Chris A double? Two beds? I suppose you wouldn't share?
Dickon Well, I . . .
Lindsey Now, just a moment . . .
Chris I've left it late—and honestly, I can't find a *dog kennel*. And you must know what it's like on campus these days . . .
Dickon (*quietly*) Yes.
Chris Well, then . . . ?
Dickon It's up to Mrs Ashe. Dear lady, could we perhaps see the room?
Lindsey Well, I really hadn't considered—very well. You'd better come in.

>*Chris and Dickom disappear from window*

Lindsey turns into the room

>(*Half-amused, half-exasperated*). Well, well . . . !

>*Dixon and Chris enter through the door*

Dickon Oh—it's even better inside. The beams and that fireplace. Do you burn logs? And just look at that china? What is it?
Lindsey A dessert service—Davenport. One of my treasures. (*She goes past them to the door*) The staircase is through that door opposite. Go up and see the room—right on the landing.

>*Dickon and Chris go out*

>(*Calling*) There's only one place you'll have to duck—just at the top . . .

There is a crack

Chris (*off*) Ouch!
Lindsey (*laughing*) Well, I *did* warn you.
Chris (*calling*) There's bags of space—couldn't be better . . .

Act I Scene 2

The telephone rings. Lindsey calls off

Lindsey Excuse me. Settle it between yourselves and we'll talk it over. (*She picks up the telephone*) Westfield three-seven . . . Marsh? . . . Gavin Marsh? (*She pauses*) The Housing Office? Oh. No, I'm sorry, but I'm afraid I can't . . . (*There is a long pause*) Yes—you certainly have left it late, but there must be *somewhere*. Surely the University has—no, really I haven't even a corner.

Dickon and Chris enter

Chris If it's all right with you . . .

Lindsey holds up a warning hand

Lindsey Now listen—please. I've already two students here—and I . . . (*Another pause. Slowly*) Well—if it's like that—it is? Then there *is* an attic—but I do *mean* attic . . .

Dickon and Chris exchange glances

Chris (*softly*) There's a TV too. Do you think she'd let us watch football?
Dickon (*watching Lindsey*) S-hush.
Lindsey I see. Oh, dear, in that case—come and see me. Have you got transport? A motor bike—oh heavens! No, no. When will you come? *Now!* Oh, just a moment . . . (*She pauses, then takes the receiver from her ear, looks at it, then replaces it. She turns and looks at the boys. Despairingly*) And what Mrs Bevil is going to say, I just don't know!

Beaming, Dickon and Chris shake hands with each other, as—

the CURTAIN falls

SCENE 2

The same

Lindsey is at her desk, wearing her spectacles and typing. She rips letter from machine and sits back reading it aloud, or her recorded voice is heard

Lindsey My dear Millicent: I have waited before breaking the news. My three students moved in five weeks ago. They are Dickon, Chris and Gavin—who is called Blitz, apparently because his politics are both red and warlike. They are not as worldly as they would like to think—but they are young and gay, and I feel we may deal pleasantly together without personal involvement. I hope the view over the kitchen garden continues pleasant. Your affectionate sister—P.S. Reassure Cedric that I use the word *gay* in its archaic sense. (*She pauses, laughs, then takes a pen and scribbles*) P.P.S. Who wants—to know anything—about a dishcloth—anyway! (*She puts an envelope in machine and starts to type*)

There is a knock at door. She goes on typing. Knock is repeated

(*Calling*) Yes?
Chris (*off*) Could we see you for a moment?

Chris enters with Dickon and Blitz behind him. Blitz is a contrast, with large spectacles and a beard. He has a very slight Cockney accent

About the rules?
Lindsey (*only half attending*) Rules—(*she stops typing and turns*)—can't we just make them up as the occasion arises?
Blitz Organization is essential both inside and outside industry.
Lindsey Oh. Actually I *am* trying to be industrious myself just now—I suppose you'd better come in. Sit down somewhere.

Blitz closes the door. Lindsey puts letter in envelope and stamps it

You'll find some sherry over there. Help yourselves—someone get me a glass.

She swings her chair rovnd and takes off her spectacles. The boys pour sherry, there is a buzz of conversation as glasses are passed—"Thanks", "Cheers", etc. Dickon and Chris sit on the settee. Blitz stands by the bookshelves

And why this sudden urge for discipline? We seemed to be coping quite satisfactorily so far.
Dickon Well—you *were* a little—*edgy*—last night . . .
Lindsey I merely pointed out that it was somewhat injudicious to scrawl across the bathroom mirror "Bev rules O.K."
Chris (*straight-faced*) We're all very repentant and we won't do it again.
Lindsey Mrs Bevil has worked for me for twenty years and we understand each other. Either treat her with respect or leave her alone. Understood?

Murmurs of agreement

Otherwise we go on as we are. One of you should be here at night. You have your rooms cleaned but you provide your own food, cook your own meals—and always leave the kitchen absolutely clear before going to bed. Any further questions?
Blitz I don't graduate for another year. When these two leave, can I have the double room?
Lindsey If you stay on.
Blitz Good show. Di will like that.
Dickon Watch it — *Speaking*
Chris Hold on, Blitz *together*
Lindsey And who is Di?
Blitz My girl friend. Will she pay the same rent?
Lindsey Are you proposing this girl friend should—I believe the current term is *shack up* with you?
Blitz Sure. You'll like Di—she . . .
Lindsey (*firmly*) No.
Blitz (*surprised*) No?

Act I Scene 2

Lindsey Again to use your own expression—no way.
Blitz Why ever not?
Dickon (*softly*) Leave it, Blitz.
Lindsey This applies to all three of you. You may certainly invite your girl-friends in for a drink—or a snack. If you want them to share your beds you must go elsewhere.
Blitz (*disgustedly*) For Gawd's sake—didn't you ever . . .
Chris Blitz . . .
Lindsey Since I enjoyed nearly thirty years of happy marriage, one may assume that I did. (*Quietly*) Sexual fulfilment is not the prerogative of your generation.
Chris (*sotto voce*) Wow!
Blitz I only said . . .
Lindsey It would be all round the village in forty-eight hours. And undoubtedly Mrs Bevil would leave—which I could not for a moment contemplate.
Blitz All right. You've made your point. And—I beg your pardon . . .
Lindsey Thank you. (*She puts the envelope on a pile of others and gets up*) I'm just going to the postbox with these. Finish your sherry and then you can wash up the glasses.
Dickon Could I go for you?
Lindsey No. I need to stretch my legs.

Lindsey goes out

Chris The old girl can pack a mean punch when she wants to.
Dickon I don't mind when she shouts. It's when she stands on the rug and goes all quiet—why do you keep calling her *old*?
Blitz Fifty-eight . . .
Dickon Fifty . . . ?
Blitz Fifty-eight. Her age. I borrowed her dictionary yesterday. It said "To my dear daughter, Lindsey Margaret on her twenty-first birthday"—and it gave the date. Like I said. Fifty-eight. Old as God.
Dickon (*angrily*) How would *you* know His age? You're an atheist!

Dickon goes out sharply

Blitz Now you look here . . . (*He starts to go after Dickon*)

Chris pulls him back

Chris Cool it, Blitz.
Blitz I won't . . .
Chris (*quietly*) I said cool it.

Blitz jerks his arm free

Blitz He's always getting at me . . .
Chris And you're always getting at him. You two can never agree—so leave each other alone.
Blitz It's all very well for you . . .
Chris Let's get these glasses done, shall we? (*He puts his glass into Blitz's hand and fetches the others. Moving to the door*) Come on.

Chris and Blitz exit

A slight pause during which Dickon's guitar is heard playing softly

Lindsey enters. Before shutting the door, she stands listening to the guitar. Then she goes and sits at the desk

That's better. Now—(*she puts on her spectacles and picks up some papers*) —what's next. Ah—Phillip . . .

She sits back with a letter in her hand, reading. Phillip's recorded voice is heard

Phillip Dear Lindsey. If I am to show *Love Me Long* to Regius Films, I need the finished manuscript in the next six weeks. We shall be all right for Blaine's spring list—but I am just a tiny bit uncertain about the character of Rosalind. I will ring you next Thursday night—late-ish. I hope things are not too hectic. Bianca sends her love and so do I. Yours ever, Phillip.

Lindsey Six weeks! Oh God! (*She takes a sheet of paper and writes. Her own recorded voice is heard*) Dear Phillip. I will do my utmost. The plain truth is I have been solitary so long and so used to peace and my own way . . .

There is a knock at the door. Lindsey continues writing. The knock is repeated

Oh, damn—come in.

Blitz enters

(*Swinging her chair round*) Yes—what is it?

Blitz (*somewhat awkwardly*) I suppose—I suppose—I couldn't . . .

Lindsey Couldn't what?

Blitz Borrow the car this afternoon?

Lindsey The car?

Blitz I've got to get a part for the bike, and neither Chris or Dickon . . .

Lindsey Oh, all right. (*She opens a desk drawer and brings out her handbag*) I think you'll need to put in some petrol. (*She finds her car keys in her bag and throws them to him*)

Blitz Well, actually—you see my grant isn't due till Wednesday—I was rather hoping . . .

Lindsey (*resignedly*) How much?

Blitz Could you—manage—three quid?

Lindsey I should think it might be arranged. (*She takes some notes from her handbag and gives them to him*)

Blitz Thanks. And—and I could get you any shopping while I'm in the town.

Lindsey Ask me after lunch. And for goodness sake get off—I'm trying to work.

Blitz Sorry.

Blitz exits quickly

Act I Scene 2

Lindsey sighs exasperatedly

Lindsey I do dislike Saturday mornings—they all seem to be milling around—perhaps it'll be better later. (*She reads the letter*) "So used to peace and my own way . . ." (*She resumes writing. Her recorded voice is heard*) About Rosalind—I'm inclined to agree. But don't ring me on Thursday. One of my students is twenty-one and his father is taking us all to dinner at the Royal. Then we are coming back here for a final drink. I'll take a chance and ring you Friday—much love to you both . . .

There is a knock at the door

Oh, *dear*. (*Calling*) Yes?

Chris enters

Lindsey writes for a second, then turns

So . . .?
Chris Could I—could I ask a favour?
Lindsey (*meaningly*) You could certainly *ask*.
Chris Would you—just trim my hair?
Lindsey And what's wrong with the barber?
Chris It costs ninety p.
Lindsey I'll do it for forty-five.
Chris Well—actually . . .
Lindsey (*nodding*) The grant's not due till Wednesday.
Chris Something like that.
Lindsey Oh, for goodness sake! Go up to the bathroom and put a towel round you. I'll be there in a moment. (*She turns back to her desk*)
Chris Oh, *thanks*.

Chris goes out

Lindsey (*calling*) Chris . . .!

Chris puts his head round the door

Chris Yes?
Lindsey Wash it first. (*She turns back to her desk*)
Chris Sure.

Chris goes out. His steps are heard on the stairs then a crack

(*off*) Ouch!
Lindsey Serve you right! (*She signs the letter, puts it in an envelope, then sits back in her chair*) That's done. I suppose I'd better have a look at Rosalind—what did I do with . . . (*She opens a desk drawer, looks through and pulls out a manuscript in a folder*) Here we are. Page—page—where's that index. Page forty-one. (*She finds the page, settles more comfortably and starts to read*) "They were—contained in silence—as the room was itself contained. She felt all his strength flowing into her . . ."

There is a knock at the door

"My little love, he said. My very little love . . ."

The knock is repeated. Lindsey puts down the folder. She draws a deep breath

Who is it this time?

Dickon comes in

Dickon It's me.
Lindsey So I see. (*Politely*) In what way may I assist you?
Dickon This dinner on Thursday. I shall have to wear my suit . . .
Lindsey I should hope you don't intend to go in your jeans.
Dickon The pants are split.
Lindsey Again! What on earth do you—oh, all right. Leave them in my bedroom. I'll see to it.
Dickon *Dear* lady . . .
Lindsey Out! (*She turns to her desk*)
Dickon I only wanted to say . . .
Lindsey Out! (*She reaches for a ruler*)
Dickon (*hastily*) Yes, ma'am.

Dickon goes out

Lindsey *Wretched* boys! (*Reading*)—"Rosalind—my little love . . ." For heavens sake—how could anyone possibly fall in love with a creature like Rosalind!

There is a loud burst of radio, off. Lindsey gets up.

(*Deliberately very quiet*) I shall go stark staring raving *mad*. (*She goes to the door, opens it and calls*) Chris! Dickon! Turn it down! Do you hear—turn it down!

Chris (*off, cheerfully*) Do you want it right off?
Lindsey No. (*Suddenly*) Yes—yes. Right off. (*The radio stops dead*) Thank you. (*She shuts door and turns back into the room*) I must say I didn't foresee anything like this. (*Laughing suddenly*) How Millicent would gloat! Anyway—perhaps I can do something about that beastly woman on page forty-two. (*She begins to pace the room, working it out*) If I switched chapter four—the wedding scene—and then brought the seduction bit—wait! That might just do it—let's see. (*She hurries to the desk and picks up the manuscript turning the pages*) Yes—it *could* work. If I . . .

A motor cycle suddenly begins to rev and roar. Lindsey slaps down the folder

This is *too much*! (*She goes to the window and pushes it up. Calling*) Blitz! *Blitz!*

Blitz (*off, at a distance*) Hullo?
Lindsey STOP THAT NOISE . . . !

The noise stops abruptly

I should think so!
Blitz I got to test her, haven't I?
Lindsey Well, take it over to the garage—it won't sound so loud.

Act I Scene 2

Blitz I can't—the back wheel's off.
Lindsey (*angrily*) Then you can ruddy well *carry* it! (*She bangs down the window*) This is ridiculous—I must control myself. (*Pausing*) I think I need alcohol. (*She pours a glass of sherry, drinks some, then returns to desk, putting the glass beside her. She starts to read again, and relaxes, drinking more sherry*)

A brief pause, then Mrs Bevil's furious voice is heard

Mrs Bevil (*off*) Never! Never in all my born days . . .

Mrs Bevil flings open door and enters

Mrs Ashe—I'm through!
Lindsey (*turning*) Bev!
Mrs Bevil This is *it*! I'm leaving.
Lindsey But what is the matter? And why are you here on a Saturday morning?
Mrs Bevil Bevil dug some broccoli for you—and seeing it ought to be et fresh—so I come up—and there's gratitude I must say . . .
Lindsey But what's the *matter*?
Mrs Bevil I come up the path and what do I see? That Blitz a-dragging his bike across the lawn—cutting it all into racks—and Bevil taking so much trouble to keep it nice . . .
Lindsey Bev—it's my fault. I told him . . .
Mrs Bevil And that's not all. Have you seen my kitchen? Because if not, you're coming to see it right now.
Lindsey Bev . . .
Mrs Bevil Black oil on the tiles and on the wall—and all them filthy rags soaking in my sink . . .

Blitz appears at the window

Blitz (*cheerfully*) Hullo—what's up?
Mrs Bevil What's up! You ask me what's up! (*Beside herself*) My kitchen —all that *oil*!
Blitz All right—all right. Don't get your knickers in a twist . . .
Mrs Bevil Don't you speak to me like that—you dirty-minded young bastard!
Blitz Here—steady on . . . (*He swings over the window on to the seat*)

Dickon and Chris enter at the same moment. Chris is wearing only shorts and drying his hair on a towel

Dickon⎫ What's happening down here . . . ⎧*Speaking*
Chris ⎭ Is it a revolution . . . ? ⎩*together*
Mrs Bevil (*to Chris*) And you can keep out of it . . .
Lindsey Stop it!
Mrs Bevil I've not forgot how you left the bathroom on Tuesday ..
Lindsey (*raising her voice*) QUIET!

There is silence

I'm very sorry, Bev. But we didn't expect you and it would have been cleaned.
Blitz I'm waiting to clean it now—if she'll move her old flat feet . . .
Mrs Bevil If you don't watch it, I'll put one of those flat feet where you won't like it!
Blitz Oh, cool off!
Lindsey Please . . .
Mrs Bevil I'm going. And take your mucky pants off them cushions.
Blitz (*suddenly, getting up*) And you should have gone long ago—the pittance she pays you.
Mrs Bevil Well! If everyone's to be told what money I get . . .
Blitz I don't know *what* she pays you. I do know it isn't thirty pounds a week.
Mrs Bevil Thirty pounds—you're out of your mind.
Blitz Anyone who doesn't earn thirty pounds a week should go on Social Security.
Lindsey Blitz!
Mrs Bevil Now you listen here—sonny. Me and Bevil has the pension and what we make lawful outside it. And we won't never ask no Government for anything but what's our due . . .
Blitz And while you work for peanuts, others have to do the same. Can't you see you're being *exploited*?
Mrs Bevil All I can see is that I've worked happy here for twenty years—and now its come to this. (*She goes to the door and opens it*) I'm right sorry, Mrs Ashe—but it's me—or them. (*She goes through the door and turns*) And you can't say I didn't warn you.

Mrs Bevil goes, closing the door

There is a pause. Lindsey looks at the boys

Lindsey (*quietly*) I hope you all know what you've done.
Blitz Oh—she doesn't mean it . . .
Lindsey (*still quietly*) You heard what she said. "Me or them." Well, it's certainly not going to be "them".
Dickon (*blankly*) You mean—you're throwing *us* out?
Lindsey By the end of next week.
Blitz You can't . . . ! ⎫
Dickon I wasn't even down here . . . ⎬ *Speaking together*
Chris What are we going to *do* . . . ⎭
Blitz You can't do this. We have our rights.
Lindsey And I have the right to say who I want in my house.
Chris (*reasonably*) We're well into term, Mrs Ashe. How'll we get fixed up?
Dickon It's victimization. I'll inform the Housing Office.
Lindsey Don't bother. I'll do it for you. (*She crosses to the door*) And now you can all come and clean up this mess.

Lindsey goes out

Dickon turns on Blitz

Dickon (*deadly quiet*) You—you *colossal* fool. Why did you have to bring your blasted politics into it!

Act I Scene 3   13

Dickon goes out

Blitz (*angrily*) So what did *I* do.
Chris It's just unfortunate. She wasn't expected on a Saturday—and you *did* go on a bit.
Blitz Don't you start!
Chris And it looks as though we're out of a very comfortable set-up. (*Turning*) Come on—let's get cleared up.
Blitz I've a good mind to clear *out*. Now.
Chris (*turning at the door*) Oh, no, you don't. After all, it *is* your bloody oil.

Chris goes out

Blitz pauses. Then he aims a vicious kick at the window seat and follows Chris, as—

the Curtain *falls*

Scene 3

The same. Early morning

The Curtains *are drawn. Lindsey, wearing a housecoat, comes in. She yawns, then goes and switches on the electric kettle. Dickon enters, wearing a dressing-gown*

Dickon (*cautiously*) Hullo.
Lindsey (*shortly*) Good morning.
Dickon You're—up early.
Lindsey I want my coffee.
Dickon May I do it?
Lindsey No.
Dickon You *are* mad at us, aren't you?
Lindsey Yes. (*She spoons coffee into mugs*)
Dickon Look—suppose she agreed to come back—with us still here . . .
Lindsey Suppose the moon fell right out of the sky?
Dickon Last night—I went to see her . . .
Lindsey (*turning*) You did *what*? (*Pausing*) What did she say?
Dickon Actually—I did most of the talking.
Lindsey (*grimly*) So I can imagine.
Dickon She sort of—just looked.
Lindsey I can imagine that, too.
Dickon It was damned hard going.
Lindsey The mind boggles. What *could* you have said?
Dickon Oh—how much you needed her—after so long. And then that we were *grovelling* sorry—and had the greatest respect for her—(*suddenly angry*)—dash it all—I did everything but go down on my knees and bang my head on the floor—stop laughing!

Lindsey "Oh, pardon me, thou bleeding piece of earth—"
Dickon "—that I am meek and gentle with. . ." Meek! I'll say I was meek. I tell you, lady, friendship can go no further.
Lindsey Didn't she say *anything*?
Dickon Oh, yes. "Thass—"
Lindsey "—thass as maybe."

The kettle whistles. Lindsey pours water into the mugs. She gives one to Dickon

They stand for a second drinking. Dickon wanders over to the window-seat

Dickon There's something else I ought to tell you.
Lindsey Something . . .? Dickon, what else did you say?
Dickon Well—I had to lay it on a bit . . .
Lindsey (*ominously*) Dickon . . .
Dickon I said—I passed your room last night, and I—heard you sobbing quietly into your pillow.
Lindsey Dickon!
Dickon I thought it rather a nice touch.
Lindsey I could kill you!
Dickon (*looking out of the window*) Not for the moment—I think she's coming up the drive—with a thumping great bunch of flowers on her handlebars.

Lindsey hurries to the window. A bicycle bell tinkles

Lindsey Upstairs—quick! No—take your coffee.

Dickon moves to the door

And if you must listen—at least keep quiet.

A door shuts, off

Go on! Quickly!
Dickon Okay—okay.

Dickon exits

Lindsey hurries to her desk. A pause

Mrs Bevil enters. She wears a winter coat over her apron, and a fearsome little knitted hat

Mrs Bevil (*grimly*) Morning. (*She draws back the* CURTAINS *at the two windows*)
Lindsey Good morning, Bev. I was—just making some coffee.
Mrs Bevil (*turning*) Oh, well—if I'm to find I'm not wanted . . .
Lindsey No, no. (*Suddenly*) Oh, Bev, dear—I'm so glad to see you.
Mrs Bevil Then you get back to your bed, and I'll bring up your tray. Cooked? Or just toast?
Lindsey (*moving to the door*) Just toast, please. And fresh coffee. And if we have any honey . . .

Act I Scene 4   15

Mrs Bevil Of course we got honey. I don't let things get runned out.
Lindsey Thank you, Bev.
Mrs Bevil Go on, then. I haven't got all day. (*She collects the mugs on a tray*) And why are you using this powdered stuff? Haven't we got any graduals?

Lindsey goes out

(*Looking after her*) Sobbing into the pillow indeed!

Mrs Bevil picks up the tray and crosses to the door, as—

the CURTAIN *falls*

SCENE 4

The same night

The CURTAINS *are drawn and the fire alight. Lindsey is at her desk writing under a table-lamp. A soft chiming clock strikes the last quarter and then three. Lindsey looks at her wristwatch, then resumes writing. Voices are heard, off. She pauses, listening, then gets up, crosses to door left, half opens it and stands listening. Dickon is heard talking incoherently, then he cries out*

Chris (*off*) Dick—what's the matter? Half a minute—I'll put the light on. Here—wake up! Come on—wake up. It's Chris.
Dickon (*off*) The s-sheeted d-dead ...
Chris (*off*) The *what*? You're having a nightmare.
Dickon (*off*) I'm s-so c-cold.
Chris (*off*) No wonder—all the bedclothes on the floor. Here—get under the blanket—I'll go down and make a cuppa.

Steps are heard coming downstairs. Lindsey opens the door

Lindsey (*quietly*) Chris ...

Chris, in his dressing gown, enters.

Chris Sorry I woke you. Dickon's had a bad dream. I'm making a drink.
Lindsey Come in here—it's warmer. I could do with one myself.

They move to the desk. Lindsey switches on the kettle

Chris Have you been working late again?
Lindsey One has to—with a deadline to meet. (*Pausing*) Chris—about Dickon. Do you think he's—stable?
Chris (*laughing*) Good lord, yes. A bit emotional perhaps. Hasn't quite left it all behind yet.
Lindsey Left what behind?
Chris The adolescent bit.

Lindsey (*laughing*) Oh, Chris, *dear*! You're six months younger. Are you over it?
Chris (*simply*) I'm not bothered.
Lindsey Lucky old you.
Chris And don't forget—he's got his finals in June.
Lindsey So have you. Aren't you bothered about that, either?
Chris I may sweat a bit the last few weeks. The way I look at it—you do the work and get good marks. Or you don't work and you get what you deserve.

Dickon comes in. He is in pyjamas and barefooted, shivering slightly

Dickon H-hullo.
Chris Dick—go back to bed.
Dickon I'm too c-cold. (*He moves to the fireplace*) Can we put a log on?
Lindsey All right—just for a few minutes. You're shivering—where's your dressing-gown?
Chris I'll get it.
Lindsey No—there's a big rug in the chest in the dining room—that'd be better.
Chris Sure.

Chris goes out

Lindsey Sit down—no, I'll see to the fire. You sit down. And *calm* down, too.

Dickon sits on the settee. Lindsey puts a log on the fire

Dickon I'm s-sorry.
Lindsey You'll feel better when you're warm—

The kettle boils. Lindsey goes and makes coffee in the mugs

Chris comes back with a large rug

Chris Here we are—get this round you. (*He envelops Dickon in the rug*)
Dickon Th-thanks.

Chris takes two mugs from Lindsey, and gives one to Dickon. They all drink. Dickon suddenly laughs shakily

"Here will we sit—before a dying fire—"
Lindsey "—and tell sad stories of the death of kings"? Not at this hour in the morning—I'm much too tired.
Chris If you two are going to start quoting, d'you mind if I go to bed? Anyway, I *do* have an early lecture—and you make me feel a proper ignoramus.

Chris goes out with his mug

Dickon laughs shakily again

Dickon He doesn't know how often we make our quotes up ourselves.
Lindsey No need to disillusion him. Drink that and get to bed.

Dickon There's something I must tell you.
Lindsey Another time, another place . . .
Dickon No—now. Please. (*Suddenly*) It's all so hopeless—so hopeless . . .
Lindsey (*crisply*) Dickon! Stop wallowing.
Dickon Wallow . . .

Lindsey sits down in the desk chair, facing him

Lindsey Working up a nice little personal drama—and enjoying every minute of it. You'll pour it all out and go to bed relaxed and happy—and I'll be left like a drained cistern.
Dickon (*not listening*) The sheeted dead . . .
Lindsey What?
Dickon My dream—rows and rows—just shapes, no faces—and a frightful bell booming too late—too late . . .
Lindsey (*keeping it light*) Yug!
Dickon So what was in my subconscious . . .
Lindsey In your stomach.
Dickon My . . .?
Lindsey All that grisly mess you cooked up for your supper. Honestly—when I think what gets concocted on my stove . . .
Dickon I have to talk to you. Will you hold my hands?
Lindsey They'll be warmer under the rug.
Dickon My last year at school—I had a breakdown. I was in a psychiatric place for a year—E.C.T.—the lot.
Lindsey Hard luck.
Dickon Aren't you—even sorry?
Lindsey My sympathies are with your parents.
Dickon My mother died when I was two. My father—he said all the conventional things—pull yourself together—only you can help yourself. Actually, I think . . .
Lindsey (*abruptly*) What started all this?
Dickon I don't know.
Lindsey (*exasperated*) Oh—*come* on!
Dickon I don't—really I don't. I suppose—pressures. (*Abruptly*) Aren't *you* going to say the usual things—that inevitable bit about a wasted life?
Lindsey And the waste of public money which provides your grant.
Dickon My grant is minimal. My father's a rich man. (*He laughs*) He's Bellamy—of Bellamy's Brass.
Lindsey And how rich is rich?
Dickon He owns a vast works—and a sizeable chunk of the North. And me—I'm the young master wot's going to take it all over.
Lindsey Then I can't see you have anything to worry about.
Dickon Last year I tried to kill myself.

A pause. Lindsey does not speak

Are you shocked?
Lindsey Curious. I suppose you want to tell . . .

Dickon I got over the first part. And I looked forward—God, how I looked forward to University—everything going—people to talk to . . .
Lindsey What went wrong?
Dickon I suppose I found—I'm a natural solitary.
Lindsey I'm one myself now. There are certain compensations—
Dickon Not for me. So—I got in with the drug lot.
Lindsey Oh, Dickon! You're not still . . .
Dickon No, no. It didn't go very far, anyway. So I had treatment—and then I was solitary again. One can't work all the time.
Lindsey No, one can't . . .
Dickon And then—one night—it all went clean over the top of my head and I swallowed a whole lot of my anti-depressant pills. (*He laughs*) Unfortunately, a "whole lot" wasn't enough and they rushed me to hospital . . .
Lindsey Where I hope they taught you a harsh lesson with a stomach pump!
Dickon It might have been better—and quicker—if they had.
Lindsey How do you mean?
Dickon There was this young doctor—he said, "I don't know what you've taken, you young fool—but I do know you're not dying. So you'll lie and sweat it out till you can name the drug, and then I'll give you the antidote." God—he was *tough*.
Lindsey And did you sweat it out?
Dickon All the whole long night. My jaws were so stiff I couldn't speak—and I shook like I was being racked . . .
Lindsey You're wallowing.
Dickon Oh, yes—sorry. So next morning I managed to write down the name of the drug and he gave me the antidote.
Lindsey And what did your father say this time?
Dickon He never knew. I wouldn't let them tell him.
Lindsey But, Dickon . . .
Dickon So now you see what it's meant to me to come to this place. (*Abruptly*) Will you throw me out?
Lindsey No. But you must make me a promise.
Dickon Not to do it again.
Lindsey Not to do it here. (*Lightly*) I don't particularly want to find you like the sheeted dead in my back bedroom. Nor do I want to break the news to your father.
Dickon (*matter-of-factly*) Oh, you don't have to worry—the police will do that.
Lindsey (*laughing in spite of herself*) Oh, Dickon—the stark simplicity of your generation.
Dickon I'll promise, but you'll have to help me.
Lindsey How?
Dickon I'm still taking the pills. If I give you the bottle, and you hand out the prescribed dose . . .
Lindsey No.
Dickon No?

Act I Scene 5

Lindsey No. You've fought through two crises, and you'll fight your way out of this. And don't hide the bottle. Keep it where you can see it. And don't be a fool.
Dickon You're not in the least sympathetic—
Lindsey Why should I be? You're obviously a survivor.
Dickon —but I think you understand. (*He yawns hugely*) I say—I'm exhausted. What's the time?
Lindsey Half-past three. I wonder Blitz hasn't protested.
Dickon Oh, Blitz hasn't come in yet.
Lindsey Not in—at this hour?
Dickon Oh, he often stops out nights. Didn't you know?
Lindsey I did not. The girl-friend, I suppose?
Dickon Yes. Lucky old Blitz—getting it regular.
Lindsey What is she like?
Dickon Di? Well—if you ever see them together, she's the one with short hair. And I'll tell you something else. Politically speaking—you think Blitz is red. Believe me, beside her he isn't even the palest coral. (*He gets up, pulling the rug closer round him*) May I go to bed now, please?
Lindsey (*ironically*) Pray don't let me detain you. Good *morning*.

Dickon goes to the door and turns

Dickon You've been very kind. And patient. Thank you,

Dickon goes out

Lindsey You poor stupid child. Of course I would like to hold your hand and say all the useless comforting things. And what good would that do either of us. (*She gets up*) Sentiment has no part in my life now. (*She pauses, finishing her drink. Slowly*) Or has it?

CURTAIN

SCENE 5

The same. Evening

Before the CURTAIN *rises, a recording is heard—preferably at the back of the audience—of a hotel string orchestra playing a waltz. Then it breaks off—there is a drum roll and "Happy Birthday" starts. It is sung by the diners and the voices of Lindsey and the boys are heard—"Happy birthday, dear Dickon, happy birthday to you". When it ends there is a burst of clapping, then the orchestra recommences and fades out*

The CURTAIN *rises on laughter and conversation. Lindsey, wearing a long dress, is on the settee, Dickon perched on end below her, Blitz in the desk chair and Chris on the window-seat. Horace Bellamy stands in front of the fireplace. He is a handsome well-dressed middle-aged man and speaks with a Northern accent. Dickon and Chris are in dark suits with white shirts. Blitz has retained his uniform denim jacket and trousers, but for once they are neat and pressed and he has condescended to wear a tie. They all have drinks, and Bellamy is smoking a cigar*

Bellamy —and I must say, Mrs Ashe, it's been a right pleasure to have you with us. My boy speaks that highly of you in his letters—
Dickon (*embarrassed*) Father . . .
Bellamy —though he does say you have to give them a bit of stick now and again.
Dickon (*under his breath*) Oh, God . . .
Lindsey (*very quietly*) Be quiet. (*To Bellamy*) Let's just say, Mr Bellamy, that the instinct of survival is very strong.
Bellamy (*laughing*) Well, if my lad ever gets you down, either throw him out or let me know. I hope all of you realize how lucky you are.
Chris You don't have to remind us, sir.
Bellamy Good. Well now, has everyone enjoyed their evening?

Chorus of "Grand", "Marvellous", "Thank you", etc.

Then there's just one last little ceremony. Mrs Ashe—if we might . . .
Lindsey Of course. Blitz—fill up the glasses. And thank you for the brandy. Mr Bellamy. You've been more than generous.
Bellamy Thank Dickon, Mrs Ashe. It's his evening.

Bellamy pauses with his cigar poised and Chris passes him an ashtray

Ah, thank you, lad. (*He deposits his cigar*)

Chris replaces the ashtray. Blitz fetches a brandy bottle from the shelves and moves round refilling their glasses. He returns to the desk chair

Are we all ready, then? Well, as I've just said, Dickon, it's your evening. Here's health and happiness.

They all raise their glasses and toast Dickon. "Dickon—health and happiness—", etc.

Dickon Th-thank you.
Lindsey (*in a very low voice*) For God's sake, smile.
Bellamy Stand up, lad. Stand up and let's see you. You'll not be twenty-one again.

Dickon stands up

Dickon Th-thank you all very much.
Bellamy That's it, then. (*He puts his glass on the desk*) Now. (*He takes out a wallet and finds an envelope in it*) Your cheque. As we agreed.

Dickon goes and takes it

Dickon Thank you, Father.

Bellamy holds out his hand and Dickon shakes it

Bellamy You get the car later—when you finish your degree and come home.
Lindsey A car!
Bellamy Nice little Audi automatic. Brand new.
Chris You lucky devil!

Act I Scene 5

Lindsey I can't wait to see it.
Bellamy Oh—no sense in racketing about in it down here. And if he takes it over when he joins the firm, he can run it on expenses straight away—did you say something, Gavin?
Blitz No.
Bellamy Haven't said much all evening, have you? One of the quiet ones, perhaps?
Dickon Blitz—quiet? You should hear him at the Union.
Lindsey } Dickon ... { *Speaking*
Chris } (*quietly*) Easy, Dick ... { *together*
Dickon I only said ...
Lindsey (*firmly*) This brandy is delectable—so much nicer than an ordinary sweet liqueur.
Chris (*following the lead*) I went to a monastery once—in France—where the monks make a special liqueur of their own—
Lindsey —with herbs and honey? Near Anjou, isn't it? I've been there with my husband.
Chris They all looked so busy and peaceful—I very nearly joined them and gave up my degree.
Bellamy And what are you studying?
Chris Biology.
Bellamy And what'll you do when you've graduated?
Chris (*slowly*) I begin to think—it will be medicine.
Lindsey Chris—how splendid.
Bellamy Yes, indeed. Worthwhile. And you, Gavin? What are your plans?
Lindsey } Blitz isn't sure ... { *Speaking*
Dickon } Father, could we ... { *together*
Blitz (*abruptly*) I'm reading politics. And I'm going to work for the Party.
Bellamy Parliament, eh? Ambitious, are you? Got your sights on Cabinet Rank?
Blitz The Socialist Workers' Party.

There is a little silence

Lindsey (*quietly*) Blitz, dear, this *is* a birthday celebration.
Bellamy (*good-naturedly*) No, no. Just one thing I'd like to know before we leave it. What are you—you personally—working for?
Blitz The structure of a classless society.
Lindsey Blitz, I insist we do not ...
Blitz (*harshly*) The bosses must be destroyed.
Bellamy (*still good-naturedly*) Well, I'm one of them. How will you destroy me? (*He sits on the settee*) By violence?
Blitz If necessary.
Bellamy Would it surprise you to know I'm a Socialist?
Dickon (*scornfully*) You?
Bellamy Ay, me. And a strong Union man as well. I recognize the men must have representation, and we need the unions. The thing is to use them as little as possible.
Blitz How do you mean?

Bellamy Now you listen to me, young Lenin. I'm Bellamy—of Bellamy's Brass—and do you know what I always say?
Dickon (*sotto voce*) Oh, no . . .
Bellamy I say—I make good brass and it makes good brass for me. (*Laughing*). How's that? It makes good brass for me.
Blitz You mean it makes good profits.
Bellamy I employ nigh on two thousand men. What do I pay them with? Buttons?
Blitz Money has no place in a properly constituted . . .
Bellamy We've one of the best records for labour relations in the North. And why? Because any one of those two thousand knows he can sit opposite me at my desk, and talk it out man to man.
Blitz Negotiation. Not direct confrontation. The bosses are the enemy . . .
Lindsey Blitz, once and for all, this is enough.
Bellamy Nay—he's a right to speak up for what he believes in. I can see why they call you Blitz. (*Laughing*) So come now—have another drink from your enemy's profits, and let's declare a truce.
Blitz If you don't mind—I'd rather . . .
Lindsey Blitz—Chris—(*She gets up*)

The men all rise

—it's been a very good evening, but it *is* after midnight. I'm sure you probably have a few things to do before bed.
Chris Of course, Mrs A. (*To Bellamy*) Good night, sir. Thank you again.
Bellamy Good night, lad—and good luck.

Chris and Bellamy shake hands. Chris moves to the door

Chris Blitz?

Chris slightly inclines his head towards the door. Blitz puts his glass on the desk. He glances towards Bellamy

Blitz Thank you. Good night.

Blitz goes out with Chris

Bellamy (*smiling*) Good night—young Lenin. (*He moves to the fireplace*)
Dickon Look—I'm . . .
Lindsey Would you put the car away? The keys are in the ignition.
Dickon I just . . .
Lindsey I don't like leaving it out at this time of the year.

Dickon goes out

Mr Bellamy—I simply can't apologize enough . . .
Bellamy That's all right, Mrs Ashe. When a lad's got a fire in his belly, steam must come out somewhere. He'll do. (*He sighs*) I could wish my boy had a bit of fire in him.
Lindsey He has his own kind of fire. He's just a little over-sensitive as yet.
Bellamy Perhaps that's it. (*Slowly*) We had—a bit of trouble earlier on.
Lindsey He told me. I hope you don't mind.

Act I Scene 5

Bellamy No. You seem to have some—some feeling for him. And it's kind of you to let him spend Christmas under your roof.
Lindsey Spend Christmas . . .
Bellamy I'll miss him of course. But next summer he'll be home and settling down for good.
Lindsey Mr Bellamy—I know it's not my business. But may I say something?
Bellamy I'd appreciate it.
Lindsey Don't rush Dickon. There's plenty of time. Just—don't rush him.
Bellamy I'll try. But—I think you can see how it is with us.
Lindsey (*quietly*) Yes.
Bellamy There's nothing I wouldn't do for the boy. But we don't seem to communicate, chalk and cheese, Mrs Ashe. That's how it is with me and Dickon—chalk and cheese . . . (*He breaks off, looking at his wristwatch*) But there. I won't worry you with all that. I must get back to the hotel—I've some papers to look through—and a Board Meeting tomorrow afternoon—you do understand, don't you?
Lindsey Yes. (*She goes to the window and pushes it up. Calling*) Dickon! Your father's leaving. (*She closes the window*)
Bellamy I'll say good-bye then. (*He takes her hand*) I meant it when I said it's been a pleasure. And I'm glad the boy'll be with you a bit longer.
Lindsey Thank you.

For a moment they stand smiling at each other, then Lindsey turns and goes out. Bellamy follows

Voices are heard off: "Good-bye", "Good-bye, Father", Good-bye, Mr Bellamy", etc. A car is heard driving away, footsteps return to the house, the front door is closed

Lindsey enters, followed by Dickon. She is quietly angry

I am ashamed of you. You behaved disgracefully.
Dickon (*quietly*) I can't help it. He makes me cringe.
Lindsey He does everything possible to make you happy.
Dickon In *his* way. That business at the hotel tonight—the orchestra—happy birthday—how d'you think I felt—standing there . . .
Lindsey A small gesture in return for a cheque. And a car.
Dickon A car *he* chose. A dinner *he* arranged. I might have liked a concert. Or the opera. But no—I didn't have a choice . . .
Lindsey And by the way, what's this about spending Christmas here?

She sits on the settee. Dickon moves to the fireplace

Dickon He told you? May I? Please?
Lindsey As I feel at the moment—no.
Dickon I'm sorry I've upset you. Will you forgive me?
Lindsey Why should I? You and Blitz between you have spoilt the evening.
Dickon At least Blitz could talk to him. That's more than I can.
Lindsey *Why* can't you?

Dickon He's so—so absolutely *black* and *white*.
Lindsey If you mean he's firm, direct—and predictable—I agree. There are worse characteristics.
Dickon I'm more—more comfortable—when people are a bit—smudged round the edges.
Lindsey Oh, don't talk nonsense. Don't you realize—can't you *accept*—that he loves you?
Dickon He only loves his brass.

Lindsey looks at him for a second

Lindsey (*quietly*) That's the most horrible thing I've heard this evening.
Dickon I'm sorry.
Lindsey So you've already said. It's getting boring. (*Getting up*) I'm going to bed. Your present's over there.
Dickon My present . . .
Lindsey On the desk.

Dickon goes to the desk and picks up a parcel

I saved it to round off the evening. Not much left to round off, is there? Goodnight. (*She starts to move to the door*)
Dickon Wait. Please don't go like that. At least let me open it . . .

Lindsey turns back Dickon opens the parcel

Records. (*Pausing*) Oh, *glory*! The *Messiah*!
Lindsey You mentioned you wanted it.
Dickon You make me feel awful. Is there *anything* I can do to prove how sorry I am?
Lindsey (*slowly*) There might be.
Dickon Anything.
Lindsey Your father isn't leaving till midday tomorrow. You can get up early and go over to breakfast with him.
Dickon I . . .
Lindsey You'll thank him for the dinner. Be warm and charming—as you can when you wish. Talk about your work—and his. And take him a bottle of brandy. You can pay for it out of your cheque.
Dickon It won't work. I'll try. I'll try to exhaustion and beyond. We'll end up as divided as the Red Sea.
Lindsey Dickon! (*After a pause*) Do it.
Dickon (*slowly*) If I at least try, could there be a quid pro quo?
Lindsey Such as . . .?
Dickon Could we sit one evening, with a bottle of wine, and hear *Messiah* together?
Lindsey We'll think about it.
Dickon Thank you. (*Suddenly*) May I kiss you?

Lindsey pauses. Then she laughs and crosses to him, holding out her hand

No. Not your hand.

There is a pause

Act I Scene 6

(*Quietly*) It *is* my birthday.

Another pause. Lindsey laughs again

Lindsey Then here. Chastely—above the left eyebrow.

Dickon kisses her. He stands back, looking at her

Dickon (*very quietly*) You—smell nice.
Lindsey (*laughing*) Soap and water. (*She goes to the door and turns*) You boys should try it sometimes.

Lindsey goes out, as—

the CURTAIN *falls*

A recording of the last part of "I know that my Redeemer Liveth" from the Messiah *is played, preferably from the back of the audience. As it ends, the* CURTAIN *rises*

SCENE 6

The same. Evening

Lindsey is lying on the settee. Dickon is sitting cross-legged on front of the fire. A record player and a clutter of records is on the desk. There is a bright fire but only the desk lamp alight

Lindsey (*quietly*) Mm. *Lovely.*
Dickon (*as he goes and turns off the player*) It's *genius*. The power—the supreme confidence—and the accent absolutely firm on the musical statement—(*singing it*)—"I KNOW . . ." See? "I KNOW that my . . ." The great Handelian declaration.

The telephone rings

Hell! Let it ring.
Lindsey (*getting up*) No. I'm expecting a call from Phillip. (*She goes to the desk*) Put on "Comfort Ye . . ." (*At the phone*) Westfield three-seven . . .

The voice of Dr Porteus is heard so that the following conversation is complete

Porteus Mrs Ashe? Dr Porteus—Dean of Students, Westfield University. I believe you have a Gavin Marsh staying with you?
Lindsey Blitz? He's not here at the moment . . .
Porteus No. He's asked us to let you know he won't be back till sometime tomorrow. And I'd better just warn you—he'll be a bit battered.
Lindsey Don't say he's come off that wretched bike?
Porteus Something like that. Don't worry. We're getting him fixed up.
Lindsey Is it serious? Is he in hospital?
Porteus No, no. Just a few bruises here and there. He'll be all right. He just asked our office to ring. Good-bye.
Lindsey Thank you. Good-bye (*She puts the phone down*) Dickon . . .

c

Chris comes in

Dickon What's up? Oh—hi, Chris.
Chris Hi. (*Looking at Lindsey*) Anything wrong?
Lindsey That was your Dean on the phone. Blitz has had some kind of accident.
Dickon Oh. Is that what old Porterhouse . . .
Lindsey It's a little puzzling. Dr Porteus said they're "fixing him up". But he isn't in hospital—
Dickon I expect they've got him up in the Health Centre.
Chris (*quietly*) He's in the nick.
Dickon You didn't have to tell her.
Lindsey Tell me what? Now—look—I insist on knowing.
Chris You must have known about all the trouble on campus. The sit-in . . .
Lindsey There always seems to be trouble on campus. But the Vice-Chancellor said . . .
Chris There was a big demo in the town this morning. It got out of hand. Apparently it'll be on the regional news tonight.
Dickon I don't want to see it—or hear it! (*He turns on the player*)

"*Comfort Ye . . .*", *from the* Messiah *is heard, as—*

the CURTAIN *falls*

The music continues for about six bars, then fades. A TV news recording is heard in the audience

TV Voice —and considerable violence ensued when the students left the campus and paraded in the High Street. Terry Preston reports.
Second TV Voice (*heard against a faint background of the demonstration*) The demonstration at Westfield which was intended as a peaceful protest against increased university fees, ran into trouble when it tangled with a rival group from the National Front

The noise of the demonstration increases. Dickon's voice suddenly tops it

Dickon Turn it off! Turn the damn thing off!

The recording stops abruptly

SCENE 7

The same. Morning

The window curtains are drawn back and daylight fills the room. Lindsey is writing at her desk. A motor-cycle roars up and stops. Lindsey looks up. After a second, she goes to the door and opens it. Steps are heard off

Lindsey Blitz? (*Pausing*) Blitz?
Blitz (*off*) What is it?

Act I Scene 7

Lindsey Come here a moment, will you.
Blitz (*off*) Oh, lay off . . .
Lindsey I want to speak to you. (*Firmly*) Come in here, please.

Blitz comes in. He is dishevelled and dirty and has a badly bruised face, with a strip of plaster down one cheek

It was kind to send a message . . . Blitz! Your face . . .!
Blitz It's nothing. (*Turning*) I'm going up . . .
Lindsey It needs attention. Who dressed it?
Blitz Police surgeon.
Lindsey When?
Blitz Last night, I'll go back to the Health Centre presently.
Lindsey You're not fit to drive that cycle again today. I'll clean it up.
Blitz I said . . .
Lindsey I don't care what you said. You're under my roof and for once you'll listen to me.
Blitz Oh, for God's sake . . .
Lindsey Go and sit over there—on the settee—no, don't argue. I'm going to fetch some lint and disinfectant. (*She turns in the doorway*) In the circumstances I don't think it's too early for a brandy. Help yourself—there's still some of that good bottle—if you're not too prejudiced against the donor.

Lindsey goes out

Blitz, limping slightly, gets himself a brandy

Lindsey returns, carrying a bowl and towel and a packet of lint

Come along—over here.

Blitz sullenly puts the glass on the desk and sits on the settee. Lindsey puts the bowl beside him

Hold that. Now—head back.

She cleans up his face. Blitz flinches

Blitz Hey—watch it!
Lindsey Sorry. Just keep still. I'll not touch the bit that's been stitched. (*She takes a fresh piece of lint, talking as she works*) Blitz—what happened this morning? In Court?
Blitz Fined and bound over. Nothing else the fools could do.
Lindsey But what about the University?
Blitz They may try disciplinary action—as they call it. Then they'll really see what a demo's like.
Lindsey Oh, Blitz—why? You're not violent by nature.
Blitz If people won't listen, it *must* be violence.
Lindsey (*suddenly angry*) You make me tired. What do any of you really know about violence?
Blitz We know more . . .
Lindsey . . . A few demos and punch-ups with the police. Did you ever walk

down a street with houses burning on both sides—people trapped—and more fire screaming down out of the sky . . .

Blitz Oh, if you're going to bring your piddling little war into it . . .

Lindsey We fought our little war—as you call it—for you lot. What are we getting in return?

Blitz We want justice—equality—freedom from starvation—oppression . . .

Lindsey Do you think we don't want all that? But I've seen improvements in my lifetime—it moves slowly. You want it all yesterday.

Blitz Yesterday. Tomorrow. Fifty years. The final breakthrough must come.

Lindsey The great and glorious revolution. And when we've all died on the barricades, and you've hosed the streets clean of blood—what then?

Blitz It's no good talking to you—you and people like old Bellamy. You don't know what goes on in the world—you haven't even read the books . . .

Lindsey I think you underestimate us.

Blitz And when you've finished your ministering angel bit—I suppose you'll tell me to go.

Lindsey No.

Blitz Why?

Lindsey Because you're free to believe what you like. And because I think that under that hard red shell there's a decent boy trying to get out.

Blitz You're pompous and patronizing—

Lindsey —and as old as God. I know. (*She straightens up*) There. That should feel better, even if you won't admit it. (*She collects the bowl, etc.*) Now you just lie quietly on your bed and plan your revolution, and I'll send you up some good strong coffee. (*She moves to the door*)

Blitz Damn your coffee! You know what you can do with it!

Lindsey (*laughing*) At the price it is today! No way, man. No way!

Lindsey goes out, still laughing

Blitz gets up

Blitz Oh, hell (*He limps to the desk and picks up his half-finished brandy*) Why won't they realize—it drags on and on . . . (*He tosses off the brandy. Suddenly he puts his hand to his eyes*) I'll never see it in my lifetime—what shall we *do* . . . (*He drops into the desk chair. He bows his head on the desk and sobs harshly and quietly*)

Lindsey comes in. She pauses as she sees him, then goes out again

Lindsey (*calling, off*) Bev—will you be so kind as to take up the coffee as soon as its ready? And perhaps you could fix a sandwich?

Mrs Bevil (*off*) I'll do that.

Blitz gets up, wiping his sleeve over his eyes. He moves across to the door

Lindsey enters, meeting him

Blitz pauses

Blitz (*gruffly*) Thanks.

Blitz goes out

Lindsey sighs. She crosses to her desk, puts on her glasses and picks up a letter. Millicent's recorded voice is heard

Millicent My dear Lindsey: Would you care to spend Christmas with us? We have given up open fires and installed gas central heating which Cedric considers more hygienic. On Boxing Day the Bennetts will be coming in for bridge. How is your game these days? We do hope the students will not be returning in the New Year—surely you suspected that boy was a Communist? Your affectionate sister . . .

Lindsey puts down the letter. She pulls a sheet of paper towards her, picks up a pen and writes. Her recorded voice is heard

Lindsey Dear Millicent: Thank you—but no, I shall not be spending Christmas with you. Dickon is staying here—at his own request. I expect we shall play a lot of records and drink vast quantities of wine. Of course we knew Blitz was a Communist. We found the hammer under his bed, but the sickle has not turned up yet. Happy Christmas! Your affectionate sister . . .

The recording fades, as—

the CURTAIN falls

Scene 8

The same. Evening

A recording is played of "The Holly and The Ivy"—preferably on a guitar with a singer, and in the audience

The CURTAIN *rises on subdued lighting: a big log fire and the desk lamp. Lindsey, wearing her housecoat is lying on the settee. Dickon is sitting in front of the fire, apparently having just stopped playing his guitar. He gets up, puts it on the desk, then goes to the fire and puts on logs. The lighting comes up a little. Lindsey sits up*

Lindsey Dickon—be careful! You'll incinerate us . . .
Dickon (*laughing*) "Man is born to sorrow as the sparks fly upwards . . ."
Lindsey You weren't born to anything but luxury.
Dickon Luxury?
Lindsey Good education. Assured job. Money. And no doubt—eventually—a good marriage. Incidentally, when are you going to get yourself a steady girl?
Dickon Oh—women. D'you want some more wine?
Lindsey Please.

He goes to the shelves and pours wine

Don't you like women?

Dickon Of course I do. Don't you think I'm normal?

Lindsey I admit that on the several nights you've stayed out, I didn't assume you were studying.

Dickon That? (*He brings her a glass of wine and squats before the fire, drinking*) Calculated gratification of a biological urge.

Lindsey You cold-blooded young monster!

Dickon Not at all. I just haven't found what I'm looking for.

Lindsey Do you know what you're looking for?

Dickon (*slowly*) Someone I can talk to—intelligently—afterwards. (*He leans forward and kicks the log on the fire*)

Lindsey Yes, that is quite important. Dickon—don't keep disturbing those logs!

He turns suddenly, putting a hand on her knee

Dickon (*abruptly*) When the flames shine on your hair, it is the colour of autumn leaves.

Lindsey (*complacently*) Royal Chestnut.

Dickon (*puzzled*) Sorry . . .?

Lindsey *Royal Chestnut.* That's what it says on the bottle those autumn leaves come out of.

Dickon jumps up

Dickon (*angrily*) You exasperating, irritating woman! Won't you ever—for a single unguarded moment—allow yourself to be sentimental?

Lindsey Only in my books. (*Laughing*) Some people say they drip.

Dickon Well, I've read two and I don't agree.

Lindsey Have you, now? And what did you . . .

Dickon You cater for a specific market. You take a romantic story and thereafter write a straightforward piece of English on a given subject.

Lindsey You are going to become a *most* distinguished literary critic . . .

Dickon You have also sold film rights. You must be a rich woman.

Lindsey Rich! Take away agents' commission, expenses and the taxman and I can just about keep my ears above water.

Dickon So don't submerge them for a moment—I want to give you your Christmas present.

Lindsey Present? You've already given me about two gallons of expensive perfume. Dickon—I hope you haven't spent any more money.

Dickon This hasn't cost anything. (*Abruptly*) I've made you a song.

Lindsey And I'm going to hear it now?

Dickon There's something I ought to tell you first. It started in my mind when I first came. You were sitting in the garden—in the autumn air. Quiet and very peaceful . . .

Lindsey Actually, I remember I was . . .

Dickon (*not listening*) I thought: no more fuss and fret—at the end of her life . . .

Lindsey Now, just a moment . . .

Dickon And I wondered if it was really like that. No emotions. No regret.

Act I Scene 8

I made the song. Listen. (*He fetches his guitar, sits down in front of fire, half back to the audience, and sings the theme song "The Soft September Air". At the end of the song he pauses*) "Oh—how desire doth outrun performance."

Lindsey Don't say that. It is charming.

Dickon Perhaps it's not so bad musically. If only I could write poetry. It's so unfair—if Wiley can, why can't I?

Lindsey Who is Wiley?

Dickon In the maths department—a dreary old Professor—about as sensitive as—as one of his own slide rules. And he can write good poetry—and get it published.

Lindsey How do you know it's good?

Dickon There was a bit in a Sunday paper. I memorized it—listen.

Lindsey Do we want to hear . . .

Dickon Listen "The fire of passion does not leap. It burns with a slow and incandescent flame. And in the heart of all this fury, there lies a diamond. Cold as stone and bright as death. And that—is love."

Lindsey (*quietly*) And that—is poetry?

Dickon Yes.

Lindsey I see what you mean. Will you believe me when I say I prefer yours?

Dickon Why?

Lindsey Professor Wiley makes a positive statement. You take a thought and develop a musical theme. With charm—and sentiment.

Dickon Sentiment . . .!

Lindsey Sentiment. I love your song and I am honoured that you wrote it for me. May we hear it again?

Dickon Now?

Lindsey Please.

Dickon plays the opening bars. He begins to sing

Dickon The soft September air
       Lies cool and still
       All passion spent . . .

The CURTAIN *slowly falls*

ACT II

Scene 1

The same. Afternoon
Lindsey is at her desk, typing. She rips the sheet from the machine and sits back, reading. Her recorded voice is heard

Lindsey Dear Phillip: You are right—I never knew a year go so—so *breathlessly*! Today Chris and Dickon have gone up to University to hear the results of their finals, and Blitz is out somewhere—probably behind a banner. So for the moment it is blissfully peaceful. Now—about the new book...

A motor-cycle arrives and stops. Lindsey pauses, looking up, then turns her chair and takes off her spectacles

(*Calling*) Dickon...

Steps are heard off

Dickon...?

Dickon puts his head round the door

Dickon I'm going upstairs to cut my throat.
Lindsey (*politely*) Please use the clothes line. It will be much less messy.

Dickon withdraws his head. A pause. Then he enters

Dickon (*abruptly*) I got a Third.
Lindsey Congratulations.
Dickon On a Third! It's tantamount to a failure.
Lindsey Nonsense. You can write B.A. after your name.
Dickon Who cares?
Lindsey I do. And so does your father. He'll be so proud at the ceremony.
Dickon He isn't coming.
Lindsey Oh, Dickon—why not?
Dickon He has to go to Brussels. (*Bitterly*) The E.E.C. can't spare him.
Lindsey But surely...
Dickon The young master will wear a cap and gown and touch hands with the Chancellor. For the old master it will be business as usual. Long live Bellamy's Brass.
Lindsey Just for once could he delegate?
Dickon He has. He suggests you come with me.
Lindsey I should like that. I've never seen a degree ceremony. And afterwards, we can have our own celebration.
Dickon Oh, he's prepared to celebrate. He's coming down on Tuesday

Act II Scene 1

before he goes to Brussels. We seem to have made a breakthrough. He actually asked me what I would like.
Lindsey And have you told him?
Dickon Not yet. It depends on you.
Lindsey On me?
Dickon I would like us to dine here. In the cottage—

Chris's sports car is heard arriving

—just the three of us. With a white lace cloth and all the silver—and to eat our dessert off the Davenport service. And if you think that's childish, you have only to say so.
Lindsey This evening we'll sit down together and plan the menu . . .

A door bangs off

Chris (*off*) I say! (*Nearer*) I've got a First!

Chris bursts in

I've got a RUDDY FIRST!

Dickon turns abruptly up by the window-seat

Lindsey Oh, Chris—I'm so glad.
Chris I can't believe it—I honestly didn't expect . . . Oh, Dick, I'm sorry—how did you get on?

Lindsey gives him a quick warning glance

Lindsey He got a Third. So now you can *both* put B.A. after your names—and that's three years of your lives accounted for. Now—how about opening a bottle . . .

Dickon comes abruptly down into the room

Dickon It was that blasted *viva* did it—anyway, Chris—congratulations.
Chris I thought you said the *viva* was a walkover. So what did happen?
Dickon There were three of them. Old Porterhouse—I don't mind him. And Fisher. And the external examiner. I never knew his name. Mouth like a plum. Unripe.
Chris You should have been sound enough on your subject—you're always . . .
Dickon Oh, it was fine at first—just routine stuff. Lawrence—and Russell. And then this—this plum character says, "Mr Bellamy, would you expound . . . Expound! I ask you! "Would you expound for a few moments on Shakespeare's political views?"
Lindsey Now that is interesting. (*She sits on the settee*)
Dickon It's ludicrous! Shakespeare never had any political beliefs.
Lindsey Oh, what do you base that . . .
Dickon For God's sake—you're a working author. Where would he get the time?
Lindsey Time?
Dickon All that output—years of it. Magnificent immortal verse—written by hand with a quill pen—page after page—often by rushlight . . .

Lindsey But indications in the text? *Julius Caesar?*
Dickon That was history. Oh, he gave his *characters* politics—but *he* was above it. He *had* to be. I *told* them. I even threw Arnold at them.
Lindsey Arnold? You mean ...
Dickon Arnold's Sonnet to Shakespeare. "Others abide the question—thou art free. O'er topping knowledge . . ." See?
Lindsey This I should have appreciated.
Dickon Well, they didn't. Suddenly Plum Mouth said, "An imaginative concept, Mr Bellamy. But quite inconclusive. And not what you were asked."
Chris And you said?
Dickon I said: "O there has been much throwing about of brains!" Then I bowed and left.
Chris (*quietly*) Oh, Gawd!
Lindsey But what's wrong with an imaginative concept!
Chris Dick's right, Mrs A. It isn't the sort of answer they want.
Dickon Read the set books and repeat back contents. (*Furiously*) A-academic regurgitation!
Chris Dick! Cool it! (*He goes to Dickon*) Stop shaking. Now—listen ...
Dickon I can't ...
Chris (*firmly*) No—listen. Fetch your guitar and we'll all go over to the *Magpie* and have a singsong. A few pints'll take away the taste of plums. Go on, now.
Dickon (*shakily*) Okay. S-sorry.

Dickon goes out

Chris And you're coming too, Mrs A. I'm going to buy us a succession of the finest and largest sherries in the county.
Lindsey I can certainly use them!

Dickon is heard off, playing the guitar and singing

Dickon (*Off, to the tune of* "*John Brown's Body.*")

> We're all down from the Universitee—
> We're all down—

Chris and Lindsey join in as Chris opens the door for her

Chris ⎫ —from the Universitee— ⎧ *Singing*
Lindsey ⎭   ⎩ *together*

Chris and Lindsey go out, laughing

Chris ⎫ We've got degrees, we're as clever as can be—
Lindsey ⎬ And now we want to earn some bread— ⎫ *Singing*
Dickon ⎭ Glory, glory, Allelulia! ⎬ *together*
             Glory, glory, Allelulia! ⎭
             Glory, glory, Allelulia ...

As they sing, there is the sound of the car starting up and driving away, sound and voices fading, as—

the CURTAIN *falls*

Act II Scene 2

Scene 2

A country pub

The scene is played in front of the Curtain. *A guitar is playing somewhere in the background*

> *Lindsey and Chris enter right and stand drinking and talking. Two Old Ladies, in their sixties, enter left and stand with their pints of beer. The Second Old Lady concentrates on drinking, the First Old Lady peers out into the audience, then looks round, back to the stage, and finally sees Lindsey and Chris. She nudges her companion*

First Old Lady There they are.
Second Old Lady (*peering into the audience*) Where?
First Old Lady Over there—by top counter.
Second Old Lady Oh, yes. (*She takes a sup*) So they are, then.
Lindsey (*to Chris*) I've never seen anyone so determined to get completely stoned. I wonder he can find the strings.
Chris It's only natural. The pressure's off. No more lectures, no more work . . .
Lindsey And the disappointment of not getting a first-class degree?
Chris Perhaps. But it doesn't matter for him, does it? He won't have to look for a job.

They continue talking quietly

Second Old Lady Don't dress all that smart for a writing person, do she?
First Old Lady (*darkly*) Maybe she's smart in other ways. (*She sups*) 'Tes said the one wi' guitar's her special pet.
Second Old Lady (*peering across*) That other ent so bad. (*Approvingly*) Good straight legs.
First Old Lady Wants the scissors took to 'is 'air.
Second Old Lady (*not really listening*) If a man's got good straight legs, he'll *manage*.
First Old Lady My 'usband's legs were so bowed as a billhook. (*She sups*) 'E managed.

They both continue drinking

Chris You don't have to worry about Dickon, Mrs A. Have another drink?
Lindsey Thank you—I will. (*She mimes taking a note from her pocket*) Take this. It's my round.
Chris No, no. Tonight you're our guest.
Lindsey Take it. I've a valid reason. Our cover has been blown.
Chris Our *what*?
Lindsey See those two old witches over there—under the window?
Chris The ones who keep peering at us with little sparrows' eyes?
Lindsey Sparrows! More like vultures. The self-imposed village watch committee. Rip up a reputation in less time than you can down that beer.

Chris But what do you imagine they could be saying?
Lindsey I don't imagine. I could write the dialogue. So take this. Slowly—let them have a good look.

Chris takes the imaginary note. Lindsey finishes her drink

Lindsey Right. Let's go into the lounge.
Chris Shall we offer them a drink? Or smile sweetly as we go by.
Lindsey We'll just—go by.

Lindsey and Chris exit right

Second Old Lady Wouldn't think the lads'd want someone 'er age.
First Old Lady What's age to do with it? There were a piece in the paper this week—she eighty-one and him not twenty-three. And what happen?
Second Old Lady (*it is a statement*) 'E done 'er *in*.
First Old Lady (*it is an affirmation*) 'E done 'er *in*.
Second Old Lady Ah—but did 'e do 'er *over*?
First Old Lady (*grimly*) 'E did.
Second Old Lady Then that's all *right*, then in't it? (*She starts to chuckle, and goes into a coughing fit*)

The First Old Lady helps the Second Old Lady off left

The guitar sounds more loudly behind the CURTAIN. *Voices begin to call from the audience—clapping and shouting*

Voices Hurrah! Give us a song! Come on, lad! What about a song: etc. etc.

Dickon appears before the CURTAIN *with his guitar*

There is increased clapping and cheering. He holds up his hand but noise continues.

Dickon All right—all right! Quiet, will you! (*Shouting*) QUIET!

The noise dies away

I will now sing you a little thing of my own composing—

Clapping and cheering

—a modern folk song entitled "Then and Now—"

More cheering

—and I wish to announce that the management of this hotel have—at *stupendous* expense—

Cheers and laughter. Dickon holds up his hand for silence

—at stupendous expense engaged the services of my old friend to sing the soprano part. Ladies and gentlemen! A big hand for—Mister—Christopher—CARUSO!

Frenzied applause and cheering

Act II Scene 2

Chris comes out beside Dickon and bows
Dickon plays the opening chords for silence

    (*singing*) Oh, fair maiden, sang the lover.
    How I do desire thee.
    All my passion spilleth over.
    Come, I pray you, come to me.
Chris (*falsetto*) Oh, fair sir, replied the maiden.
    If I love you as you say,
    I with child will soon be laden—

Someone in the audience calls "Shame!"

    So the answer must be nay.
Dickon Altogether—now!
Audience ⎫
Chris   ⎬ Oh, nay, sir, nay sir, nay, sir. ⎰ *Singing*
Dickon   ⎭ Oh, nay, sir. Nay sir. Nay! ⎱ *together*
Dickon (*singing*) Come on, darling, cries the lover,
    You're a woman, I'm a man.
    And our day will soon be over.
    Let's get cracking while we can.
    Though I own I'm feeling naughty,
    I'll be careful if you will.
    Said the maiden, looking haughty,
Chris (*falsetto*) Nark it, mate. I'm on the Pill!
Dickon ⎫ So the answer can be yea, sir! ⎰ *Singing*
Chris   ⎭ So the answer can be yea— ⎱ *together*
Audience ⎫ Oh, yea, sir, yea, sir. Yea sir! ⎫
Dickon   ⎬ Any time, sir. Yea, sir. YEA! ⎬ *Singing together*
Chris   ⎭ Oh, yea sir, yea sir— ⎭

Ad lib till the audience are ready to stop

    Chris and Dickon stand bowing, and finally exit behind the CURTAIN *or into the wings*

A moving car is heard, recorded and played in audience: optional—see production note. The voices of Lindsey and Chris are heard, as if they are in the car

Lindsey (*sleepily*) Chris—I want to confess.
Chris Go ahead.
Lindsey For the first time in years, I think I'm a little—just a little—drunk.
Chris How does it feel?
Lindsey Bee-yew-tiful. (*Enunciating carefully*) Floating blissfully on a tideless sea of old brown sherry.
Chris What about Dickon?
Lindsey (*matter-of-factly*) He's dead.
Chris What a bore. Can you pinpoint the exact time? We're sure to be asked at the inquest.

Lindsey He gave a sort of strangled snort about two miles back. Hold on. (*Pause*) Yes. Life appears to be extins—exht . . .
Chris Extinct?
Lindsey (*solemnly*) Thank you. I am obliged.
Chris (*equally solemnly*) Not at all. My pleasure.
Lindsey But it *is* sad—so *young*.
Chris Don't worry—it happens all the time. We'll leave him in the garage overnight and Bevil can bury him in the morning.
Lindsey His father's coming on Tuesday. How will we explain?
Chris Mm—that *is* awkward. Tell you what, Mrs A. If we keep straight on now, we could make the coast by daylight—
Lindsey —and flee the country! How splendid. I *am* enjoying this. (*Pausing*) One *small* thing—if we go straight on, how about the burial?
Chris No problem. Just watch out for a convenient ditch.
Lindsey You are a very re-source—resourceful young man. Isn't this a *childish* conversation. Funny how alcohol makes people b-bawdy—or belligerent—or childish. (*Suddenly*) CHRIS . . .
Chris What's up?
Lindsey Quick—find that convenient ditch! I think the body is going to be sick!
Chris (*singing*) Oh, nay sir! Nay sir! Nay sir!
Lindsey
Chris } Oh, yea sir! Yea sir! YEA! { *Singing together*

The car is heard revving up: laughter and singing continues then all fades out

SCENE 3

The cottage. Evening

Voices are heard, off. Lindsey, wearing a cocktail dress, enters with Horace Bellamy. Dickon follows, in his suit and a white shirt. They are all carrying small coffee cups. Lindsey switches on main lights

Bellamy —a splendid meal, Mrs Ashe. Enjoyed every minute of it.
Lindsey I'm so glad.

Lindsey goes behind the desk, puts down her cup and switches on the lamp. Dickon stands by the window-seat. Bellamy stands in front of the fireplace, drinking coffee and looking round appreciatively

Bellamy And I can see why Dickon has been happy here—a right lovely place and everything in keeping.
Lindsey Thank you.
Bellamy That china, now—must be worth something. A family heirloom?
Lindsey My godmother left it to me. I don't know about value. To me it would be irreplaceable.
Bellamy Well, I'm going to ask for the privilege of adding something. (*He finishes his coffee and holds out his cup to Dickon*) Here, lad—take this. And let's have that parcel.

Act II Scene 3

Dickon takes the cup to the window-seat and picks up a parcel which is lying there

A little "thank you", Mrs Ashe. For looking after the lad.
Lindsey Mr Bellamy, there's no need. I've enjoyed . . .
Bellamy I'm not going to say it's an antique—(*he takes the parcel from Dickon to the desk*)—but it's been specially made at our works and I've had one of my best designers on it. (*He unwraps the parcel*) There.
Lindsey It's a bird . . .
Bellamy A linnet—yes. A knocker for your front door. First you'll have to get this plate fixed—the holes are ready drilled—then he slots in here —so. And then you lift his tail and he gives the warning with his beak.
Lindsey Just look at the detail—every feather. It's perfect.
Bellamy As near as can be. Everyone got that interested. And I told them —I said "All our brass is special. This has got to be *right*."
Lindsey *Thank* you. And you, Dickon.
Dickon (*quietly*) I didn't know about it.
Bellamy No. I thought it'd be a surprise for both of you. And here's your screws for the plate—just feel the weight of those, Mrs Ashe. Every one hand made—you won't easily find the work or that quality of brass these days.
Lindsey It is a complete craftsman's job.
Bellamy And a craftsman saw it through. My works manager, Joe Heaton.
Dickon (*lightly, with the accent*) Ay, old Joe Heaton wi' is little flat 'at . . .
Bellamy That'll do. You treat Joe with respect. You'll be seeing a lot of him in the next few months. (*He takes out a cigar case*) May I?
Lindsey Please do. Dickon—find an ashtray.

Bellamy sits on the settee. As he talks, he selects a cigar, finds a piercer in his pocket and prepares the cigar. Dickon fetches an ashtray from the window-seat puts it beside his father, and stands in front of the fireplace. Lindsey sits in the desk chair and drinks her coffee

Bellamy I thought when you've taken your degree you'd like to come out to Brussels for the last two days—give you an insight into how they run these things.
Dickon Father . . .
Bellamy Or you can go off somewhere on your own if you want. But come beginning of September, we start you on the job.
Dickon Father—I . . .
Bellamy Right from foundations, eh, Mrs Ashe? A man's got to know how it's done before he can tell others to do it.
Lindsey Certainly.

Bellamy puts the piercer in his pocket and brings out his matches

Bellamy So Joe's got a short works course set out—about three months. Then you'll go through Accounts and Despatch, and have a good spell on Overseas Sales. Say eighteen months—and we should have you on the Board. How's that? (*He strikes a match to his cigar*)
Dickon (*quietly*) I'm not coming into the firm.

Bellamy pauses. He blows out the match and puts it and the unlighted cigar in the ashtray. He looks at Dickon

Bellamy (*also quietly*) Now, lad—what's this?
Dickon I said . . .
Bellamy I heard what you said. Maybe I didn't hear right.
Dickon You heard right.
Lindsey (*getting up*) Mr Bellamy I think I should leave you and Dickon alone.
Dickon I specially want you to stay.
Bellamy (*getting up*) Dickon . . .
Lindsey (*to Dickon*) Why?
Dickon You've often called me erratic—hysterical. I want you to see I'm absolutely serious. And—it will save me having to say it all twice.
Lindsey Mr Bellamy . . . ?
Bellamy I don't know what nonsense he's got in his head, but if he's not ashamed for you to hear it—and it *is* your house . . .
Lindsey Very well. (*She sits in the desk chair*)

Bellamy sits on the settee

Bellamy Now look—I'm not all that pigheaded. All these exams recently —must have been a strain. Put it down to nerves. Take a long break— take six months—then come back and we'll talk no more of it.
Dickon Six months. Sixty years. It wouldn't make any difference.
Bellamy So. You're passing up ownership of one of the biggest industrial set-outs in the North?
Dickon Yes.
Bellamy Why?
Dickon I don't want to make brass. I want to—make songs.
Bellamy Songs? (*Suddenly laughing*) Well, fair enough. I've nothing against that.
Dickon Then you . . .
Bellamy Everyone needs a bit of a hobby. Your time from nine-thirty till five is my business. What you do with your evenings and week-ends is yours.
Dickon I can't spend three-quarters of my life in a cage. I must be free— be my own man.
Bellamy Of course you're your own man . . .
Dickon No. Let me tell you something. Remember—about three years ago—you took me to the Corporation banquet . . .
Bellamy Bought you your first dinner suit. From my own tailor.
Dickon I was standing by the bar. There was a bit of a crush. Someone said, "Over there? That's Bellamy's boy."
Bellamy What's the matter with that? You *are* my son.
Dickon Don't misjudge me, Father. I've every respect and admiration for you—your great business and all your generous charities—oh, yes, you're in the running for Mayor, and eventually you'll get your knighthood . . .

Act II Scene 3

Bellamy What's all this leading up to?
Dickon I'm proud to be your son. I won't be Bellamy's boy.
Bellamy Words—words—some fool with too many gins under his belt and nowt to curb his tongue.
Dickon Must we go on like this? Can't you see my point and let me go?
Bellamy Let you go! Am I to put a life's work into my son, and then just see him walk away from me?
Dickon Not from you. From what you stand for.
Bellamy It's same bloody thing, isn't it!
Dickon I've tried to tell you for years. I could never make any impression.
Bellamy Now—plain and straight. You mean this?
Dickon Yes.
Bellamy All right—but I'll not see you go down. If you don't fancy what I've made for you, you can tell me what you do fancy. I'll set you up in it and you can do it your way—
Dickon Please . . .
Bellamy —but it'll have to be on a proper basis. You'll have to make it pay.
Dickon Thank you, Father. But no.
Bellamy (*angrily*) Then what the hell *are* you going to do?
Dickon The world's a big place. I'll find something.
Bellamy A drifter. A drop out. And see here. My brass may offend you, but there's another kind and you'll need it. It's called money.
Dickon I'll manage.
Bellamy What on? Manna from heaven?
Dickon If it falls.
Bellamy (*jumping up*) You wicked ungrateful young swine!
Lindsey (*quietly, getting up*) Mr Bellamy . . .
Bellamy It's too much. Tell him to get out of my sight. (*He moves away below the settee*) I never want to see him again. (*He stands with his back to Dickon*)
Dickon Father, I'm sorry . . .
Lindsey (*very quietly*) Dickon . . .
Dickon I must . . .
Lindsey Go upstairs.
Dickon One thing . . .
Lindsey Just go upstairs.

Dickon looks at her, then at his father, who still has his back to him. Then he goes quickly out

Bellamy (*turning*) By God—this is a facer.
Lindsey Just a moment.

She goes to the shelves and pours two brandies. He stands in front of the fireplace. She brings him the glass

Drink this—no, don't talk just yet. Drink it down.

He tosses off the brandy. She takes his glass back to the shelves and sits on the settee with her own drink

Better?

Bellamy Thank you. (*He retrieves his cigar and matches from the settee*) I apologize for losing my temper.
Lindsey As you said—it's a facer.

Bellamy lights his cigar and throws match into the fireplace

Bellamy What am I going to do?
Lindsey (*gently*) I think you'll—have to let him go.
Bellamy When I look at him tonight—I can't believe he's my flesh and blood. He's got nothing of me—nor his mother neither.
Lindsey I *had* wondered about that.
Bellamy Whether he were like Anne? Lord, no. Fine strong lass, she was. Cut above me socially. County people. Father Lord Lieutenant . . .
Lindsey I see.
Bellamy Always full of life. And that forthright. "Bellamy", she'd say—called me Bellamy— d'ye see? Couldn't bear Horace. "No-one can say I married you for your money. I wonder why they think I took you?" But she knew. And so did I.
Lindsey How long were you married?
Bellamy Five splendid years. Then Dickon. (*Slowly*) Who would have thought—a strong healthy lass like that—wasn't built for child-bearing.
Lindsey So that was it.
Bellamy Ay. Never picked up. Said, "There's your boy. Bellamy. Take care of him. I'm not going to give you another." Then—two more years. Watching her slip away from me.
Lindsey Does Dickon know this?
Bellamy Nay. I wouldn't want him told. (*Pause*) Have you any children?
Lindsey By the time we gave up hoping, we were too old to adopt.
Bellamy So you've taken my boy—and the others—to your heart.
Lindsey I didn't think there would be this involvement—tell me, did you ever consider marrying again?
Bellamy (*moving to the desk*) Not after what was between me and Anne. (*He puts his cigar butt in the coffee saucer on the desk and turns to her*) I'm no saint, Mrs Ashe. I admit that. (*Quietly*) But in all these years I don't think any woman's been the worse for what she might have given me.
Lindsey I can believe that.
Bellamy Forgive me for rambling on—but it's been peaceful—sitting here in this beautiful room. And you're a good listener.
Lindsey I wish I could do more.
Bellamy I'll be at the Royal till nine tomorrow morning. If he likes to come over—well, the door's open. No more than that. Will you tell him?
Lindsey Yes.
Bellamy Thank you. (*He glances at his watch*) And now, if I might use your phone, I'll ring Masters to fetch me.
Lindsey (*getting up*) I'll drive you back.
Bellamy There's really no need.
Lindsey I'd like to. And I don't think you should be alone—may I make a suggestion?
Bellamy Please do.

Act II Scene 3

Lindsey I'll drive you back, and we'll have another drink and perhaps some coffee. Then you'll take two of my tablets—they're only mild but you must have *some* sleep.
Bellamy True.
Lindsey And once you're on that plane tomorrow, you won't have much time to brood—at least not for a day or two. Right?
Bellamy Right. (*He moves to her*) You know, Mrs Ashe—you're a right good lass yourself. (*Quietly*) A right good lass.

They look at each for a second. Lindsey smiles

Lindsey (*quietly*) Thank you.

Lindsey goes out. Bellamy follows

A pause, then a car is heard starting and driving off. Another pause

Dickon enters, goes and switches on the electric kettle. A second later Blitz puts his head round the door. He is barefooted and wears a short towelling dressing-gown

Blitz You making coffee?
Dickon (*shortly*) Yes.
Blitz Make enough for two. (*He goes to the settee, and stretches out on it, yawning*) You're privileged. We odds and sods have to make it in the kitchen.
Dickon Oh, shut up.
Blitz What's up with you? (*He glances over*) Had a row with your old man?
Dickon How did you . . .
Blitz Heard him shout his head off. Then you rushed upstairs. I suppose they've been chewing it over. Anyway, they've gone off now.
Dickon Both of them?
Blitz Saw them from my window. Went in her car. What's he done? Cut you off with a shilling? Or just pinched your girl friend?
Dickon (*slowly*) What the hell do you mean? (*He comes over to Blitz with an open jar of coffee in his hand*)
Blitz Oh, lord—don't blow your top over nothing. You must have heard the talk . . . Watch out, you're spilling that—here, let me. (*He takes the coffee from Dickon and goes over to the kettle*)
Dickon What did you mean?
Blitz Nothing—always gossip in villages. Round the cottages—in the pubs. Doesn't mean a thing—just a laugh . . .
Dickon Gossip about what?
Blitz Oh, come *on*. Everyone knows she's your girl-friend. Nothing wrong with that—if you like 'em mature.
Dickon You—you filthy little beast!
Blitz Now hold on! I was only needling you . . .
Dickon Saying such vile things—and with no possible reason . . .
Blitz (*defensively*) Well, you've always been friendly—and you were here for those three weeks at Christmas.

Dickon It's—it's ridiculous. (*Quietly*) Apart from anything else—she could be my grandmother.
Blitz Of course she could. So that's it, isn't it? Nothing to get in a state about.
Dickon (*quietly*) And what do you really think?
Blitz It doesn't matter what I think. Anyone wants to enjoy themselves, I'm all for it.

The kettle boils. Blitz makes coffee in mugs

Dickon You and your rotten ideas. You—you drag people down—reduce them. You *smear* everything—
Blitz You're taking it all too seriously. Look—I'm sorry. I shouldn't have told you.
Dickon Well, you have told me, haven't you? So it's too late. (*He pauses*) Th-that's what the b-bell said . . .
Blitz What're you on about. What bell?
Dickon In m-my d-dream. Too l-late . . .
Blitz (*suddenly alarmed*) Dickon! Don't look like that—it's all right. Sit down—and drink this—you're shivering . . .
Dickon (*backing away*) G-get away f-from me . . .
Blitz Dickon—listen . . . !
Dickon Damn and blast you!

Dickon runs out

Blitz Dickon—wait! (*He puts the coffee mug on the desk and turns to the door*)
Chris (*off*) What's the devil d'you think you're doing. Dickon!

Chris runs in

What's happening? Dick's just gone past me like a bat out of hell.
Blitz How was I to know he couldn't take a joke?
Chris What kind of a joke?
Blitz Nothing. Nothing. I think he's out of his mind.

A motor-cycle revs up violently. Chris turns to the window and pushes it up

Chris (*calling*) Dickon—wait! Come back—!

The motor-cycle roars away. Chris shuts the window. Blitz moves to the door

Blitz! What have you been saying to him?
Blitz Oh, lay off, can't you! Poor little rich boy—with his car and his doting dad—well, I could tell you something . . .
Chris Just tell me what you said to him.
Blitz The hell I will . . . !

Blitz runs out

Chris Blitz!

Chris runs out after Blitz, as—

the CURTAIN *falls*

Act II Scene 4   45

After a moment, a spot comes up on the CURTAIN, *C. A telephone rings, off*

Chris comes through the CURTAIN *and mimes picking up the receiver. Dr Porteus' voice speaks from off-stage, so that the complete conversation is heard*

Chris Westfield three-seven.
Porteus Is Mrs Ashe there? Dr Porteus, Westfield Uni . . .
Chris Oh, Dr Porteus—Conway here. Chris Conway? Is it about Dickon?
Porteus Yes, He's . . .
Chris I've been out looking for nearly two hours—just got back actually. Is he on campus?
Porteus He's in Westfield General.
Chris I knew he'd come off that bike . . .
Porteus A nightwatchman found him in an empty storeroom. He's taken a massive overdose . . .
Chris Overdose? My God—he's not . . .
Porteus They're working on it. Does Mrs Ashe know where we could find his parents? We tried his home but there's only an answering machine.
Chris His father's down here—at the Royal. *And* Mrs Ashe.
Porteus Oh, good. I'll ring . . .
Chris Just a moment. Are you at the hospital?
Porteus Yes.
Chris I'll go and fetch them over. Where will we find you? Casualty?
Porteus Reception. Park Street entrance.
Chris I'll get going.
Porteus Thank you. Chris . . .
Chris Yes?
Porteus Don't panic them. But step on it.
Chris Right. (*He mimes replacing phone, and exits through the* CURTAIN)

SCENE 4

A hospital casualty department

The scene is played in front of the CURTAIN

Bellamy, then Lindsey, then Chris enter, from the wings each carrying a folding chair of the black-leather-and-chrome type. They set them up and sit. Lindsey is wearing a light wrap round her shoulders. They do not move

A telephone rings. Staff Nurse Kelly comes through the CURTAIN. *She is about thirty, and carries a large folder under one arm. She mimes taking the receiver from a wall-type phone*

Kelly Casualty. Staff Nurse Kelly speaking. Dr Grieves? . . . Oh—she's got an emergency at the moment . . . Yes, yes . . . Oh, yes, sir . . . Ten o'clock? I'll tell her. Thank you. Good-bye. (*She mimes hanging up the phone*)

Dr Grieves enters through the CURTAIN, *followed by Sister. The doctor is in her late twenties, wears a white coat, spectacles and a stethoscope round her neck. She is wiping her hands on a towel. Sister can be any age, pleasant, capable*

Dr Grieves All right, Sister, he'll do now. Ruddy young fool. Yes, Staff?
Kelly Mr Fell says can you see him in his room at ten o'clock tomorrow morning.
Dr Grieves Ten o'clock! Just when am I supposed to sleep! Oh, all right. D'you think you could rustle me a cup of coffee out of the machine?
Kelly If I'm asked nicely.
Dr Grieves I'm asking you nicely.

She throws the towel to Kelly who catches it

Kelly It's on its way. Sister—I got that file from records.
Sister Thank you, Staff. (*She takes the file*)

Dr Grieves yawns

Kelly Black no sugar?
Dr Grieves (*through the yawn*) Blacknosugar.

Kelly goes out through the CURTAINS

That's it, then, Sister. Get him up to the ward for the night—what's left of it.
Sister (*looking at the file*) Yes. Doctor. (*To herself*) Ah . . .
Dr Grieves And tell them to throw him out before ten. Can't fill up beds with cries for help. (*She turns to exit through the* CURTAIN)
Sister I think he meant it. It's the second time . . .
Dr Grieves (*turning*) It's what?
Sister I thought I recognized him when they brought him in. I sent Kelly to records.
Dr Grieves Let's have it. (*She takes file and reads*) Well—just look at this! And going back to—*why* do they do it? Everything set up for them—opportunities—(*breaking off*)—are his parents here?
Sister His father's in Reception. And a lady. I don't think she's his mother.
Dr Grieves In the circumstances, she can count herself lucky. I suppose I'll have to talk to the father. (*She glances at her watch*) Can you carry on for about ten minutes?
Sister (*laughing*) It *has* been known.
Dr Grieves Right, then. I'll go and see Dad.

Dr Grieves crosses to Bellamy and mimes speaking and giving him the file. She stands looking over his shoulder as he reads

Nurse Kelly appears through the CURTAIN, *carrying two cardboard cups*

Kelly I brought one for you. (*She gives Sister a cup and looks round*) Where's . . .
Sister She's gone down to reception. I should drink it yourself. Anything desperate out there?

Act II Scene 4   47

Kelly Old Protheroe came in about ten minutes ago.
Sister Don't tell me he's been swilling his nettle tea again!
Kelly By the look of him he's been bathing in it.
Sister Clean him up and take him to the dispensary. They'll know . . . (*She pauses*)

A distant ambulance bell comes nearer and stops

Oi-oi! Here we go! (*She raises her cup to Kelly*) Here's to the Health Service!
Kelly (*raising the other cup*) A-*MEN*!

Sister and Kelly swallow their coffee and exit quickly through the CURTAIN

Dr Grieves straightens up taking the folder from Bellamy

Dr Grieves It's your decision, Mr Bellamy. If you won't see him, you won't.
Bellamy He wouldn't let them tell me the first time. Why should I see him now?
Dr Grieves He not only needs your support. He very definitely needs professional help.
Bellamy He'll get all the help he asks for. But I'll not see him.
Dr Grieves Then we'll send his records to your own doctor, with our recommendations. I'm afraid there's nothing more we can do here.
Bellamy Thank you. I'm sorry you've wasted your good time—and your experience—on someone who isn't worth it.
Dr Grieves (*quietly*) You've had a considerable shock, you may feel differently later. I hope so, anyway. And you'll have to excuse me—(*going*) —I've several other customers waiting—good night.
Bellamy Good night.

Dr Grieves turns and exits through the CURTAIN

Lindsey (*quietly*) I wish you would change your mind—
Bellamy No.
Lindsey Dr Grieves is right. He does need help.
Bellamy I should have been informed the first time—by the medics—the University. That record—drugs—the lot! And I didn't know. I *should* have been told.

Chris goes out left, taking his chair with him

Lindsey Can't it go to his credit that he tried to spare you?
Bellamy And then does it again? A second time—that's what gets me. Couldn't come to his own father. And why? Because he was ashamed. Ashamed—and weak—and worthless.
Lindsey No—not worthless. He has a good brain—
Bellamy —which can't even keep him out of trouble.
Lindsey Try and understand—it's not unusual. He does have a good brain. Unfortunately his character hasn't matured with it.
Bellamy You mean he hasn't the discipline to use his intelligence. All we pay for their education—and they can't learn that.

Lindsey (*quietly*) It isn't easy. They have a great many pressures . . .
Bellamy They've no sense of shame. They do exactly as they like and they don't *care*. And when they get into trouble they whimper, "Nobody understands . . ."
Lindsey You say Dickon has nothing of you. You both have a stubborn streak. It's a little unfair.
Bellamy What is?
Lindsey That in your case we call it character, and in his, obstinacy.
Bellamy So he can go his obstinate way. And you can't talk about unfairness, Mrs Ashe. Didn't you hear me offer him every alternative? Didn't I try everything to help?
Lindsey Yes.
Bellamy I'll do one thing more. You'll remember I gave him a cheque on his birthday? Five hundred pounds it was.
Lindsey I remember.
Bellamy Last month, my accountants told me it hadn't been paid in. Well I'm going to see it is paid in. He'll have five hundred pounds to tide him over—
Lindsey Don't you think . . .
Bellamy —and that's the last penny he can look for from me. Let him live on his songs.
Lindsey (*slowly*) No-one has—so far—considered he might write *good* songs.
Bellamy Then let him get on with it. (*Suddenly*) Eh, I'm sorry to leave you with all this. But I've got a plane to catch. Don't let him get round you any more—and promise me you'll not give—nor lend—him any cash.
Lindsey I don't think he'll ask.
Bellamy Then I'll say good-bye. (*He stands up*) (*Quietly*) You might let me know—what happens
Lindsey Yes.
Bellamy And take care.

Bellamy turns abruptly and goes out through the CURTAIN. *Chris enters left and gives Lindsey a paper cup of coffee*

Lindsey (*gratefully*) Oh, thank you, Chris. (*She drinks and sits warming her hands round the cup*)
Chris Is he coming back?
Lindsey No.
Chris Just as well.
Lindsey But surely . . .
Chris Because if he *had* wanted to see Dickon, Dickon wouldn't have seen him.
Lindsey How do you know that?
Chris I've been up to the ward. (*Cheerfully*) Just chatted up Night Sister. Smashing girl—she let me in.
Lindsey And Dickon?
Chris Just said he didn't want anything or anybody, and clamped down like a whole bed of oysters. Drink that up and I'll take you home. You must be exhausted.

Lindsey I've come through that tunnel of exhaustion—you know—where you emerge at the other end and know you'll never sleep again.
Chris By the time we get back Mrs Bev'll be due. She'll cosset you and put you to bed.
Lindsey There's Dickon to be faced. And Blitz.
Chris Want me to do it?
Lindsey No, no. Why should you.
Chris (*simply*) I'm not bothered.
Lindsey Oh, Chris . . .
Chris Mrs A.—take it easy with them. I'm sure neither of them meant it to happen like this. And—we'll all be gone by the end of the week.
Lindsey So you will. You know, I hadn't quite realized that.
Chris Going to take any more of us?
Lindsey Students? Definitely no. I'm too old for all this emotion.
Chris It passes.
Lindsey Yes, it does. Chris, you're going to make a splendid doctor. So—stable. And—not bothered.
Chris (*sitting*) This time last year, I was very bothered indeed.
Lindsey Girl troubles?
Chris No—not trouble. That's the strange part.
Lindsey How—strange?
Chris Well, there we were. The two of us. Very involved, very close. And happy. Everything was fun—and warm—and sort of *safe*.
Lindsey Yes?
Chris And suddenly—bing! Finish. Just like that. Gone.
Lindsey Did you quarrel?
Chris No, that's just it. We were still the same people—still liked each other. But we both knew it had changed. And I don't understand. That warmth—that understanding. Where did it all go?
Lindsey Perhaps—perhaps it goes into the atmosphere. And we reabsorb it —or other people absorb it. So it's used over and over again.
Chris Like matter.
Lindsey Matter?
Chris First law of thermo dynamics. "Matter can neither be created nor destroyed."
Lindsey Always there—waiting. What a consoling thought.
Chris Yes.

Lindsey laughs

Now—what are you laughing at?
Lindsey Just—suddenly—remembering. When I was eighteen and fell most passionately in love. He was over six feet tall with a big nose like Punch—and a lordly air. And all the girls fell round his feet in heaps.
Chris You never fell in a heap at anybody's feet.
Lindsey Oh, I did. And—wait for it! I was the one he picked up. Poor me—short and all puppy fat, and so poor then I had steel spectacles tied up with a bit of bootlace.
Chris I'm fascinated. Please go on.

Lindsey Alas—it was purely platonic. He'd call about twice a month and drink great cups of tea and talk about the classics. While I sat adoring—and wishing he'd come back to the present day and give me an ordinary no-nonsense kiss.

Chris How did it end for you?

Lindsey I found he was having it off with a friend of my mother's. Married with a child. So one night I shut the door in his face. Like you said—bing! Gone.

Chris Did you never see him again?

Lindsey That's the point. Thirty years, it must have been, I was married and my career achieved. And he—his feet were exactly in the same spot. He hadn't moved one inch in all those years. When I think of the good emotional matter I dissipated on him . . .

Chris Let's hope someone else used it to better purpose. (*Pause*) I *did* like her.

Lindsey The sea is full of fish.

Chris I know—but I only wanted that one little sprat.

Lindsey (*laughing*) Dear Chris—(*She drinks her coffee and hands him the cup*) I'm right—you *will* make a good doctor. Just sitting here quietly—and talking about other things—you've relaxed the tension. I shall be able to sleep now.

Chris Good. Let's get off, then—

Chris hands Lindsey to her feet and they exit left, taking their chairs with them

Scene 5

The cottage. Early morning

Di enters, crosses and switches on the kettle. She is about twenty-two, and could be attractive, but she is wearing brief pants and a man's shirt with the sleeves rolled up and open down the front, her long dark hair is greasy, and altogether she looks a mess. She stands yawning and stretching. A pause. A car drives up and stops. Voices are heard, off

Chris (*off*) I'll just put the car away. Got your key?

Lindsey (*off*) Yes. Chris—you've been such a comfort.

Chris (*off, easily*) Any time.

The car door slams. The car drives off. A pause. Then a door closes, off

Lindsey enters. She stops short

Di Hullo. Just getting some coffee. Want a cup?

Lindsey does not move or answer

What're you looking so bug-eyed about? (*She glances down at herself and laughs*) Never seen naked flesh before?

Act II Scene 5

Lindsey Certainly. But so far it has always been clean.
Di Why—you . . . !

Di runs past Lindsey to the door and opens it. Lindsey goes and switches off the kettle

Di (*calling*) Blitz! BLITZ!
Blitz (*off, sleepily*) Hullo!
Di Your landlady's back. You'd better come down—I think I'm going to slay her.
Blitz (*off*) You're what? Here—hang about . . . (*He is heard running downstairs*)

Blitz enters, and stops short. He wears only briefs

Oh, hell . . . !
Lindsey Get dressed and leave my house. Both of you.

Di sits down on the window-seat. Lindsey is very quiet

Di We'll go when we've had breakfast.
Lindsey You'll go now.
Di You going to make us?
Blitz Di—don't make a thing about it. Mrs Ashe, we didn't expect you back.
Lindsey Is that an excuse—especially in the circumstances . . . ?
Blitz Chris rang earlier (*Defensively*) Well,—he said Dickon was all right.
Lindsey So you feel your conscience is clear? Then all you have to do is pack and leave.
Di The hell he will!
Blitz Doesn't matter. I'm off next week anyway. Let's just get going.
Di What right has she to order us out!
Lindsey This is my house.
Di Your house—your this—your that. What—what *divine* arrangement says *anything* is yours? Why should you have all these possessions?
Lindsey Because I worked for them.
Di Writing a lot of damned inept books? No style, no content. No social significance . . .
Lindsey I hardly think your judgement . . .
Blitz She knows what she's talking about. Creative writing's her thing.
Lindsey And what has she published so far?
Di (*stung*) I'll publish when I'm good and ready.
Lindsey I see. Well, there are plenty of precedents for late-starters.
Di You're second-rate!
Blitz Di—leave it.
Lindsey I have never pretended to be anything else. I have an ability—note I do not even say talent—a small ability to tell tales.
Di Rubbish which should never have been printed . . .
Lindsey I have worked on that ability—stretched it—until with the grace of God and a good agent, I am able to earn a modest living.
Di You moralizing old moppet!

Lindsey And if you care to look around, I can assure you that everything you see has been bought by my pen.
Di (*getting up*) Oh, has it! You and your precious bits and pieces. You shouldn't be allowed . . .

Di turns to the cabinet and snatches up a plate. Lindsey starts forward

Look at this!
Lindsey⎫ Be careful . . .!   ⎧*Speaking*
Blitz   ⎭ Di—you're going too far! ⎩*together*
Di Fancy plates! Do you know how many people—in the other world—how many people haven't even food—let alone arty-tarty plates to put it on?
Lindsey Put that down!

Lindsey reaches for the plate. Di holds it above her head

Di (*mocking*) Nice, isn't? All flowers. "Here's a pretty thing and a very pretty thing . . . "
Lindsey⎫ Please . . .! ⎧*Speaking*
Blitz   ⎭ DI . . .!   ⎩*together*
Di And what shall we do with this very pretty thing? (*She throws down the plate, smashing it*) Oh—look at that now. Just fell out of my hand . . .

Lindsey kneels down to pick up the plate

Lindsey You wicked . . .
Di Go in pairs, I see. Better keep them together.

Di takes another plate. Blitz moves too late to stop her. She smashes the second plate to the floor beside Lindsey

Come on, Blitz—don't stand there . . .
Blitz (*catching hold of her*) No . . .

Di hands him off and sweeps the rest of china on to floor, laughing wildly. She tramples on the broken pieces. Blitz again tries to stop her. Lindsey gets up and runs forward. Di aims a kick and Lindsey falls below desk

Di—for God's sake . . .!

He struggles with Di. She goes on laughing and now screaming and trampling

Chris rushes in, with, Mrs Bevil behind him

Chris My God—what's happening . . .

He runs to help Blitz subdue Di

Mrs Bevil Mrs Ashe! Mrs Ashe . . .

Mrs Bevil hurries to Lindsey, raises her and gets her into the desk chair

Still shouting and screaming. Di breaks away and rushes out, with Blitz and Chris after her

A sound of smashing glass is heard

Act II Scene 6

Chris runs back into the doorway

Chris Mrs Bev—get the police! Nine-nine-nine! Quick! Get the police!

Chris rushes out

The shouting and smashing of glass increases. Mrs Bevil dials and speaks without waiting for an answer

Mrs Bevil Police! Police! It's Linnets Cottage, Westbury Green—send someone! Quick . . . !

CURTAIN

SCENE 6

The cottage. Morning

Chris kneels in the middle of the room, carefully collecting the broken china into a big cardboard carton. Mrs Bevil moves between the bookshelves and the desk, clearing all cups, saucers, mugs and glasses, etc., on to a tray. She is in a temper and talking non-stop

Mrs Bevil —you just tell me in your own words he said and I'll write it down. Then we'll read it over and you can sign it. Sign it! I *told* him. *Not me*, I said. I'm not signing anything without I get my glasses. (*Triumphantly*) And I didn't!
Chris (*quietly*) As things turned out it wasn't necessary.
Mrs Bevil No—and that's the whole point. Mrs Ashe must have been crazy. Letting them get away with it—all this damage—to say naught of five broken windows in the front . . .
Chris Three.
Mrs Bevil (*sharply*) Eh?
Chris She only had time to break three.
Mrs Bevil Thass as maybe. Murdering young devils. That Police Inspector was right riled with Mrs Ashe. And I don't blame him.
Chris She didn't want a fuss.
Mrs Bevil Fuss! I don't know how I kep myself back. Her standing there so quiet. "Inspector, can't we treat this as a private matter? I'm sorry you were called . . ." (*She puts the knocker in its paper into a desk drawer and shuts it with a bang*) What I can't see is why *they* couldn't do anything. They come up—they saw the damage —they took us back to station . . .
Chris I think you ought to get it clear, Mrs Bev. If Mrs Ashe wouldn't make a statement—and sign it—the police couldn't make a charge.
Mrs Bevil Charge! What did they want with a charge? They should have put them two in a cell and birched 'em till they squealed.
Chris Oh, come *on* . . .
Mrs Bevil (*vigorously tidying the desk*) And that Blitz—walking out free as air. I could right *weep*. We called the police—and what've they done? Nothing.

Chris (*quietly*) They've kept Di.
Mrs Bevil And I should just hope so! When I think of it—outside the station—in broad daylight! Kicking, screaming—smashing window of police car—and young Constable Stanley with her nails raked down his face . . .
Chris Where do you want this?
Mrs Bevil In pantry. Mind you, I think she's insane. I told the Inspector—I reckon that one's insane, I said—

Chris gets up and moves to the door with the carton

—and do you know what he said to me?
Chris (*at the doorway*) No?
Mrs Bevil He said, "Not at all, Mrs Bevil. She's what they call liberated." Liberated! What do you think about that?
Chris (*turning suddenly*) I don't know why you women keep on about liberation. As far as I can see you've all been getting your own way since the day Eve had her chat with the snake!

Chris goes out

Mrs Bevil Well . . .! Snakes indeed! (*She picks up the tray and marches towards the door*)

Lindsey enters wearing her housecoat

Oh, Mrs Ashe—what are you doing coming down? I was going to fetch you up a tray.

Lindsey crosses to the shelves and pours a drink

Lindsey I'll have it in here, Bev. You shouldn't have left me to sleep so long.
Mrs Bevil You ought to be in your bed—being knocked about like that—and I don't reckon you should take that stuff neither.
Lindsey I'm all *right*, Bev. It was only a bump on the head.
Mrs Bevil Bump on the . . .! And what'll it be next time? Burning down the Houses of Parliament!
Lindsey Bev—be a dear. Bring me a nice pot of strong coffee. (*She sits in the desk chair, glass in hand*)

Mrs Bevil turns to the door, then pauses

Mrs Bevil Bevil's boarded them windows. Says he'll be in to Westfield tomorrow and get the glass.
Lindsey Thank you, Bev.
Mrs Bevil And I've cleaned little room and put it back as 'twas. Chris cleared out Blitz's stuff and he's taking it up to college.
Lindsey Oh—how helpful. He's a very kind boy.
Mrs Bevil (*darkly*) There's some as mightn't say so. Though he's always been civil to me.

There is a tap at the door and Blitz enters

Act II Scene 6

Mrs Bevil freezes

Blitz Could I—speak to you, please?
Lindsey Come in, Blitz. Bev—would you please bring two cups.
Mrs Bevil What! After I saw them in this very room—a-crashing and a-smashing . . .
Blitz (*quietly*) I didn't smash *anything*. I was trying to stop her.
Mrs Bevil Well, it didn't look like that to *me*!

Mrs Bevil almost charges out with her tray

Blitz shuts the door and pauses

Lindsey Come and sit down.

Blitz sits on the settee. There is an uncomfortable pause

Blitz (*suddenly*) I wanted to say . . .
Lindsey Yes?
Blitz Obviously I can't come back here next term. I thought you might prefer it if I went off right away. Today.
Lindsey Have you somewhere to go?
Blitz Di's got a flat on campus. I can move in there.
Lindsey Then that might be best. Thank you—you're being very considerate.
Blitz I—didn't mean all this to happen. Dickon got things all wrong—and Di—Di just went over the top.
Lindsey I think I am a bit to blame for Di.
Blitz Oh? How?
Lindsey (*slowly*) When we got back last night—this morning—it had been a very harassed time and I was deadly tired. When I saw Di here, I was annoyed. (*Suddenly*) No. Not annoyed. *Angry*. I was suddenly so damned *angry*—I could have hit her!
Blitz But you didn't.
Lindsey But I did make some very ill-judged remarks. So I suppose—she took her revenge. And not only on me. Are the police bringing charges?
Blitz They seem to think they can.
Lindsey *Think* they can . . .! My dear boy—obstructing the police in the execution of—damaging police property—assaulting a constable—I shouldn't think there's any problem there.
Blitz We'll look after her. Someone will be along—a solicitor. I've told them to leave her alone till then. We know our rights.
Lindsey (*quietly*) Oh, yes. Hot on your rights, you lot, aren't you? Don't worry. The police have outgrown thumbscrews.
Blitz (*suddenly*) Why didn't you make a statement?
Lindsey It wouldn't have helped anything. And I think you've enough to sort out. You know—you might be better off without that young woman.
Blitz I'll stick by Di. She needs me. She's very insecure.
Lindsey One can only hope it will be worth it. (*A pause. Gently*) Is that—all?

Blitz No. (*Standing up*) I am very sorry. And I want to pay for the damage. (*Pausing*) Only . . .
Lindsey Only the grant isn't due till next term?
Blitz No, not that. I'll be working all through the vacation. If you let me know how much—only I'll have to send it to you a bit at a time.
Lindsey I don't want your money, Blitz. Forget it.
Blitz I'd rather . . .
Lindsey (*quietly*) Keep it for the Party funds.
Blitz I might have known you wouldn't understand. Well—(*he holds out his hand*)—it's good-bye then.
Lindsey Good-bye, Blitz. Good luck.

They shake hands. He turns to the door, then back

Blitz I did like being here—at Linnets.

Mrs Bevil enters with a coffee tray

Perhaps—all things being equal . . .
Mrs Bevil (*suddenly*) Equal! You talk about being equal!
Lindsey (*getting up*) Bev . . .
Mrs Bevil For I'll tell you straight to your face! Me and Bevil has brought up three sons. They haven't been to no University nor read no clever books. But they've all got good jobs and decent wives—and if I thought they had to be *equal* to creatures like you—I'd break my heart!

Blitz stands quite still for a second, then he goes quickly out

Mrs Bevil crosses to the desk with the tray, very tight-lipped

Lindsey Bev, dear—you shouldn't.
Mrs Bevil Drink this while it's hot.
Lindsey I . . .
Mrs Bevil (*still abruptly*) I'll pour it for you.

She pours coffee and hands the cup to Lindsey, who drinks meekly

Well?
Lindsey (*giving up*) Thank you, Bev—just as I like it.
Mrs Bevil Thass it, then. Now—(*she goes to the window-seat, where some china is lying*) I thought we'd put some of the best cups on here—(*she sets the cups on the corner cupboard shelves*)—and I fetched these three old plates from Bevil's family. Maybe they aren't antiques—but I thought it would look a bit less bare.
Lindsey Oh, thank you, Bev.
Mrs Bevil The other china—(*she glances at Lindsey*)—it's in a box in the pantry—you might like to see if some could be stuck.

Chris's sports car starts up and roars off. Mrs Bevil looks out of the window

And let's hope that'll be the last of *them*. (*She arranges the plates on the shelf*)
Lindsey I expect Dickon will be back.

Act II Scene 6

Mrs Bevil That's been back. Back and packed and gone.
Lindsey Gone! Bev—when?
Mrs Bevil 'Bout midday. Quiet, he was, and looked so pinched as a bone.
Lindsey But didn't he say anything?
Mrs Bevil Only that you weren't to be disturbed. And I didn't have time to listen—I were sweeping up the glass—
Lindsey But surely . . .
Mrs Bevil —and nigh on a solid hour to get the splinters out of the carpet.
Lindsey Did he leave a message?
Mrs Bevil No. (*Moving to the desk*) Have you finished with that tray?
Lindsey Yes, yes—thank you. But listen—he wouldn't go off without a word—was there a note?
Mrs Bevil Ah. Come to think of it—there *was* some words on a paper—there! I must have scrinched it up and put it out with rubbish.
Lindsey Then it has to be found.
Mrs Bevil (*defensively*) Well, it's not as if it were a proper letter—just something he wrote on a bit of an old sugar bag off kitchen counter.
Lindsey (*firmly*) Go and look.
Mrs Bevil Wait now—this just might be it in my apron pocket. (*She brings some small bits from her apron pocket, a packet of cigarettes, a paper handkerchief, a pipe cleaner—and the screwed up note. Triumphantly*) There!

She puts it before Lindsey, who smoothes it on the desk and sits looking at it

Lindsey (*quietly*) "Parting—is such sweet sorrow".
Mrs Bevil Such a fuss about a few silly words. (*She lifts the tray*) Will you be wanting me for anything else?
Lindsey (*absently*) No, thank you.
Mrs Bevil If you should—for I wouldn't say you're properly right yet—you ring Mrs Grist. Her Arthur'll bring a message into mine—land sakes—I don't believe you're listening to a word I'm saying.
Lindsey Yes, Bev, yes I am—thank you. You get along. I'll be all right. I've a lot of work to do.
Mrs Bevil Oh, all them *writings*. (*She goes to the door with the tray*) See you in the morning, then.
Lindsey Thank you, Bev.
Mrs Bevil (*in the doorway*) And when I come in, I want to find you in your bed!

Mrs Bevil goes out, closing the door

Lindsey looks at the note

Lindsey (*slowly*) "Parting—is such sweet sorrow". (*Pausing*) How wise—how very wise—to do it like this. What could we have said to each other? No sweetness—and perhaps not much sorrow. Just—sick embarrassment. (*She folds the note and puts it in a drawer*) I wonder—what will happen to him? To all of them. It's going to be lonely again. (*Suddenly*) Nonsense—loneliness is a state of mind. I wonder—should I get a cat?

No. I'm not a cat person. And they are such arrogant creatures—they've never forgotten they were gods in Egypt. I shall adjust. But—I shall miss it—all that young life flowing through the house. Good heavens—I'm wallowing! Work is the answer. Work. I'll start now. (*She takes her spectacles from the desk and puts them on. Firmly*) I'll do two thousand words—and then I'll have a brandy. (*She puts a sheet of paper in the typewriter, refers to a folder, then begins to type. She turns up the paper in the roller and looks at it*) I need another name for this woman. (*She sits back in her chair, swinging round*) Something plain and straightforward. Jane—no, that would be a cliché. (*She thinks*) Jean—Joan—Mary. Yes—no-one could cavil at Mary. Mary, Mary, quite contrary—Mary lovely Rose of Sharon—Holy Mary Mother of God . . . (*She stops. Slowly*) I wonder whether she was simple and straightforward? Well, she'd have to be, wouldn't she? She had other children to bring up besides Him. (*She swings round and types slowly for a moment, then stops*) Oh—I'm so *tired.* I can't work. I don't *want* to work . . . (*Suddenly*) Lindsey Ashe! What do you mean—you don't *want* to work! Are you or are you not a professional!

Lindsey starts to type rapidly, as—

the CURTAIN *falls*

SCENE 7

The cottage. Evening

Lindsey comes in, wearing the same clothes as in the first scene of the play, and carrying the same basket and gloves

Mrs Bevil (*off*) I'm off now.
Lindsey (*calling*) Thank you, Bev. (*She puts the basket on the window-seat, then sits at the desk*)

Mrs Bevil enters

Mrs Bevil Why *can't* you leave them weeds? Bevil'll have 'em in two minutes with a hoe. Your supper's in the oven. But I didn't make a pudding—the apple pie has to be et up.
Lindsey It shall be duly et.

Mrs Bevil goes to the desk, bringing a blue envelope out of her pocket

Mrs Bevil And Billings just brung up this.
Lindsey (*taking the envelope*) Only—the one?
Mrs Bevil That's all (*She goes to the window-seat and picks up the basket, then looks out of the window*) Right peaceful up here now, isn't it?
Lindsey I suppose it is.
Mrs Bevil A person spoke about it only the other day—no more rackety bikes a-roaring up the lane. Can't even hear the artyclateds.

Act II Scene 7

Lindsey Once you get used to being alone . . .
Mrs Bevil Alone—what's being alone! Bev's old auntie lives alone, and has done these thirty years.
Lindsey (*slightly tart*) Bevil's old auntie lives in a row of six cottages—with the district nurse on one side and the blacksmith on the other.
Mrs Bevil (*darkly*) Thass as maybe. (*At the door*) Well—see you in the morning.
Lindsey Thank you, Bev.

Mrs Bevil exits

Lindsey sits back in her chair, swinging it round

Why do I keep expecting a letter—and why should he write anyway? If he hasn't written to his father—oh, well. Let's get Millicent over. Now—where are my glasses.

She puts them on and opens the letter, reading. Millicent's recorded voice is heard

Millicent My dear Lindsey: Such a pity you could not attend Cedric's lecture on "The Ultimate Disciplines". We had a *small* but *appreciative* audience. I *am* surprised that you still hear from those *dreadful* boys! Still, the medical student seems to be progressing—fancy St Bartholomew's taking him! Of course, if he wants to visit you next month, that's your business. But really! The impertinence of that Communist to send you a postcard—and of all things—a picture of the Kremlin . . .

Lindsey begins to laugh quietly

Lindsey Actually, Millicent dear—it was Blackpool Tower—but I knew you'd prefer the Kremlin. (*She goes on reading*)

A motor-cycle arrives and stops. A pause

A young man appears at the window. He is about twenty-one, dark, good-looking, wearing jeans, a crash helmet under his arm. He has a very pleasant voice

Student Hullo.

Lindsey turns, taking off her spectacles

Are you Mrs Ashe? I'm from the University.
Lindsey Oh, no . . .
Student I've got a parcel for you. From Dickon Bellamy.

Lindsey goes to the window-seat

Lindsey Dickon! Where is he?
Student I wouldn't know. He left this with me at the end of last term.
Lindsey But that's three months ago.
Student Sure. Rum chap, old Dickon. I had to promise to bring it up on this particular day—anniversary or something. Your birthday, perhaps?
Lindsey No.

Student Anyway, here it is. (*He hands her the package*) Quite a relief—it kept getting mislaid. I say, what a glorious place—that thatch—and the pargeting ...

Lindsey Thank you.

Student And the garden—I suppose you *do* know you've got a specially fine *alnus glutinosa*?

Lindsey Alnus—oh, the alder.

Student Yes—lovely things. D'you know the Rialto Bridge in Venice is actually built on alder piles? Their native species, of course—*alnus cordata*.

Lindsey No, I didn't know. How interesting. You are knowledgeable about trees.

Student Well, I'm doing environmental studies, aren't I? Some of us have to be conservationists. This really *is* a wonderful spot. No wonder Dickon was so happy here.

Lindsey Did he say so?

Student Lord—yes. Always on about it. Could be a bit of a bore, you know, but now I've seen for myself I understand. I say—might I ask you something?

Lindsey Yes?

Student I've only got another year—finals in June. And I must move out somewhere quiet. I suppose I couldn't ...

Lindsey I'm sorry. No.

Student I couldn't—coax you? I *would* promise to behave myself.

Lindsey (*quietly*) No.

Student I should have known it wouldn't be my luck. (*Slowly*) But while I am here—would you allow me to look round the garden—just a few minutes?

Lindsey But of course.

She kneels up on seat, leans out and points off. The package slips over sill and falls outside

The boundary is that hedge down to the water meadows.

Student Bless you—hold on, you've dropped your parcel. Here you are. (*He gives it back through the window*) I won't be too long.

The Student moves off, and is heard calling back

(*off*) Did you plant the willows?

Lindsey (*calling out*) The weeper—yes. The other—(*she laughs*)—*salix alba liempede* was already there!

Student (*off, laughing*) Great!

Lindsey turns back to the desk

Lindsey Nice boy. Concerned. And reliable. (*Sitting down*) What arrogance of Dickon to ask him. I wonder what this ... (*She opens it and pulls out a wad of banknotes in an elastic band*) What ...

She puts it on desk, puts on her glasses and takes a letter from envelope, reading. Dickon's recorded voice is heard

Act II Scene 7

Dickon Dear Lady: The Mercury who brings this will not have wings upon his heels, but I think he is to be trusted. If so, you will be reading it on the anniversary of the day I came up the path and saw you sitting in your garden. I spent a year under your roof and you gave me much—but I have given you nothing until this moment. Here is five hundred pounds—all in new notes—
Lindsey (*whispering*) Dickon...
Dickon —all in new notes, for a specific purpose. Please find the finest dessert service this amount allows—and fill your shelves once more with beauty. (*Pause*) "I charge thee upon thine honour that ye do this thing." (*Pause*) What's the next line?
Lindsey Next line. "I charge thee upon thine honour..." Wait. Yes. "Sir, it shall be most honourably discharged..."
Dickon Dear Lady, I kiss your hands. Dickon. (*Pause*) One day I will write a song for you that will ring round the world.

A pause, while Lindsey sits silent looking at the letter

The Student comes to window

Student It gets more beautiful round every corner. But it is isolated, isn't it? Good thing you've got someone else in the house.
Lindsey (*turning*) Someone else?
Student Heard him singing as I came back. Plays that guitar well, doesn't he?
Lindsey Did you say—singing?
Student Yes. Perhaps you couldn't hear it in here—it *was* a bit faint. Something about autumn—September...

Lindsey does not answer

Well—I'll be going now—got to get fixed up somewhere. Pity I couldn't have come here. It's such hell on campus. (*Slowly*) I think I—could—have found peace in this place.

The Student goes away

Lindsey sits very still. The motor-cycle revs. Lindsey gets up. She goes to the window, calling off

Lindsey Just a moment...

The motor-cycle stops revving

The Student comes back to the window

Lindsey (*quietly*) The front door is at the side. Just—lift the latch. And come in.

The Student moves away

Lindsey goes slowly to the desk, puts the letter in a drawer and takes off her spectacles. She turns, facing the door. She stands quietly, waiting

Dickon's recorded voice is heard singing, to the guitar, his little song "The Soft September Air" softly in the background

Dickon The soft September air
  Lies cool and still
  Along the trees.
  All passion spent

The song is played softly to the end of the first verse only, beginning to fade on the last line but one and then dying away

  The soft September air—
  The soft September air . . .

CURTAIN

FURNITURE AND PROPERTY LIST

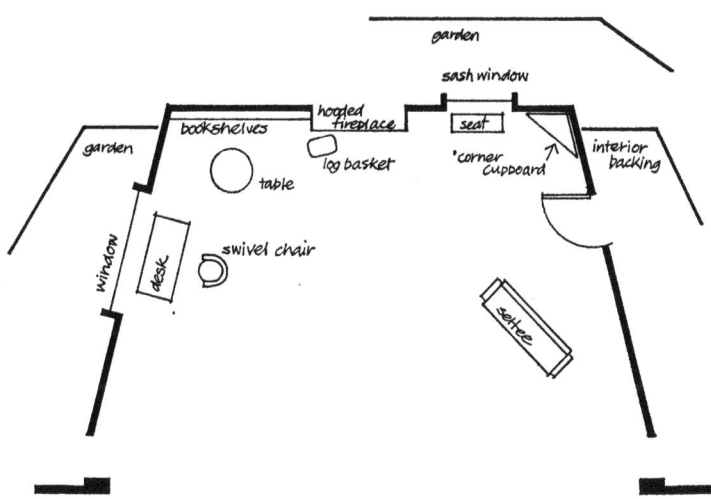

ACT I

Scene 1

On stage: Desk. *On it:* Small table lamp, telephone, portable typewriter, 2 folders of papers, pen-tray with pens, pencils, paper-knife, ruler, notepaper and envelopes in blotter, stamps, **Lindsey's** spectacles. *In drawer:* handbag with car keys and pound notes in wallet, manuscript in coloured folder
Bookshelves. Top shelves crowded with books. *On middle shelf:* silver tray with 6 sherry glasses, 6 brandy glasses, decanter of sherry
Small table. *On it:* electric kettle (practical), jar of instant coffee, 5 mugs, 3 teaspoons, sugar bowl
Wicker basket. *In it:* logs
Corner cupboard. *On it:* handsome set of green plates and dishes
Settee. *On it:* cushions
Window-seat. *On it:* cushions, ashtray
Swivel desk chair
Window curtains (open)
Sash window up

Off stage: Gardening basket with weeds, gloves, trowel, **(Lindsey)** 3 letters 1 in blue envelope **(Mrs Bevil)**

Scene 2

Off stage: Towel (**Chris**)
Personal: **Blitz:** Spectacles

Scene 3

Set: Window curtains closed

Scene 4

Set: Check mugs, coffee, kettle on table
Off stage: Rug (**Chris**)
Personal: **Lindsey:** wristwatch

Scene 5

Set: Parcel of records on desk
Brandy bottle and glasses on bookshelves
Ashtray on window-seat
5 half-filled brandy glasses for **Lindsey, Dickon, Bellamy, Chris, Blitz**
Personal: **Bellamy:** cigar, wallet with envelope, wristwatch

Scene 6

Strike: Brandy glasses, except 1 (for Scene 7)
Set: Record player and record on desk

Scene 7

Strike: Record and player
Set: **Lindsey's** spectacles on desk
Letter on blue notepaper on desk
Curtains open
Off stage: Bowl with antiseptic, lint cotton wool, towel (**Lindsey**)
Personal: **Blitz:** sticking-plaster on cheek

Scene 8

Set: Curtains closed
Glasses and wine bottles on shelves
Christmas wreath over fireplace
Off stage: Guitar (**Dickon**)

ACT II

Scene 1

Strike: Glasses, wine bottles
Christmas wreath
Set: Curtains open

Furniture and Property List

Scene 2

On stage: Nil

Off stage: 2 pint glasses of beer (**Old Ladies**)
Pint glass of beer (**Chris**)
Glass of sherry (**Lindsey**)

Scene 3

Set: Curtains closed
Mugs and small jar of coffee on shelves
Check brandy bottle and glasses
Ashtray and parcel with small ornate knocker on window-seat

Off stage: 3 coffee cups & saucers (**Lindsey, Bellamy, Dickon**)

Personal: **Bellamy**: cigars in case, piercer, matches

Scene 4

On stage: Nil

Off stage: 3 folding chairs (**Chris, Lindsey, Bellamy**)
Folder (**Nurse Kelly**)
Stethoscope, towel (**Dr Grieves**)
2 paper cups of coffee (**Nurse Kelly**)
Paper cup of coffee (**Chris**)

Personal: **Dr Grieves**: spectacles, watch

Scene 5

On stage: Set unchanged from Scene 3

Scene 6

Set: Curtains open
Check drinks and glasses
6 pleasant cups, 3 old-style pleasant plates on window-seat
Cardboard carton C
Check **Lindsey's** spectacles, files, manuscript, parcel with knocker, on desk

Off stage: Empty tray (**Mrs Bevil**)
Tray with 2 coffee cups, 2 saucers, coffee pot, cream jug (**Mrs Bevil**)

Personal: **Mrs Bevil**: apron—in pocket, cigarette packet, paper handkerchief, pipe cleaner, **Dickon's** note

Scene 7

Set: Everything, except for changes such as china in corner cupboard, much as it was in Act I Scene 1

Off stage: Gardening basket with weeds, trowel, gardening gloves (**Lindsey**)
Letter in blue envelope (**Mrs Bevil**)
Package with letter and bundle of notes in elastic band (**Student**)

LIGHTING PLOT

Property fittings required: desk lamp, wall brackets, practical electric kettle, log fire effect

A living-room, a bar, a casualty department

ACT I Scene 1 Afternoon
To open: Overall effect of bright sunlight
No cues

ACT I Scene 2
To open: As Scene 1
No cues

ACT I Scene 3 Early morning
To open: Room dim. Daylight outside windows
Cue 1 **Mrs Bevil** opens window curtains (Page 14)
Bring up to full daylight to correspond

ACT I Scene 4 Night
To open: Practicals on. Fire lit
No cues

ACT I Scene 5 Evening
To open: As previous scene
No cues

ACT I Scene 6 Night
To open: As previous scene
No cues

ACT I Scene 7 Morning
To open: Overall morning light
No cues

ACT I Scene 8 Evening
To open: Desk lamp on. Fire lit—bring up fire further as **Dickon** puts on log at opening
No cues

ACT II Scene 1 Day
To open: Overall daylight effect. Fire out
No cues

Lighting Plot

ACT II Scene 2
To open: Front cloth lighting
No cues

ACT II Scene 3 Evening
To open: Room in darkness

Cue 2	**Lindsey** switches on main lights *Snap on wall brackets*	(Page 38)
Cue 3	**Lindsey** switches on desk lamp *Snap on desk lamp*	(Page 38)
Cue 4	**Chris** runs after **Blitz** and CURTAIN falls *Bring up spot on **Chris** as he enters through* CURTAIN	(Page 45)
Cue 5	**Chris** exits *Fade to* BLACKOUT	(Page 45)

ACT II Scene 4
To open: Darkness

Cue 6	When **Bellamy, Lindsey** and **Chris** are seated *Bring up front cloth lighting*	(Page 45)

ACT II Scene 5 Early morning
To open: Brackets and lamp on, and curtains closed—drawn light outside. Fire low
No cues

ACT II Scene 6 Morning
To open: Overall morning light. Fire out
No cues

ACT II Scene 7 Early evening
To open: Overall effect of late afternoon light. Fire out

EFFECTS PLOT

ACT 1
Scene 1

Cue 1	**Lindsey** reads letter **Millicent's** *recorded voice (optional)*	(Page 2)
Cue 2	**Lindsey:** "... to say we are prepared ..." *Motor-cycle arrives and stops*	(Page 2)
Cue 3	**Lindsey:** "... lift the latch and come in." *Car arrives and stops*	(Page 3)
Cue 4	**Chris:** "Is this Linnets?" *Car door slams*	(Page 4)
Cue 5	**Lindsey:** "... just at the top ..." *Crack on beam*	(Page 4)
Cue 6	**Chris:** "... couldn't be better ..." *Telephone rings*	(Page 4)

Scene 2

Cue 7	**Lindsey** takes letter from typewriter **Lindsey's** *recorded voice (optional)*	(Page 5)
Cue 8	**Chris** and **Blitz** exit *Guitar plays softly then fades*	(Page 8)
Cue 9	**Lindsey:** "... Ah—Phillip ..." **Phillip's** *recorded voice (optional)*	(Page 8)
Cue 10	**Lindsey** writes **Lindsey's** *recorded voice (optional)*	(Page 8)
Cue 11	**Lindsey:** "... peace and my own way ..." **Lindsey's** *recorded voice (optional)*	(Page 8)
Cue 12	**Chris:** "Sure." He exits *Crack on beam*	(Page 9)
Cue 13	**Lindsey:** "... creature like Rosalind!" *Loud radio pop music*	(Page 10)
Cue 14	**Lindsey:** "... yes. Right off." *Radio stops*	(Page 10)
Cue 15	**Lindsey:** "... *could* work. If I ..." *Motor-cycle revs and roars*	(Page 10)
Cue 16	**Lindsey:** "STOP THAT NOISE ...!" *Motor-cycle stops*	(Page 10)

Scene 3

Cue 17	**Dickon:** "... flowers on her handlebars." *Bicycle bell tinkles*	(Page 14)

Effects Plot

Cue 18	**Lindsey:** " . . . at least keep quiet." *Door shuts off*	(Page 14)

SCENE 4

Cue 19	As CURTAIN rises *Soft chiming clock strikes last quarter, then "three"*	(Page 15)

SCENE 5

Cue 20	Before CURTAIN rises *String orchestra, drum roll, "Happy Birthday" singing and clapping*	(Page 19)
Cue 21	After **Lindsey** and **Bellamy** exit *Car drives off*	(Page 23)

SCENE 6

Cue 22	Before CURTAIN rises *Recording of "I Know that my Redeemer Liveth", last part.* CURTAIN *rises as music finishes*	(Page 25)
Cue 23	**Dickon:** ". . . Handelian declaration" *Telephone rings*	(Page 25)
Cue 24	**Lindsey:** " . . . Westfield three-seven . . ." *Recorded conversation with Dr Porteus (optional)*	(Page 25)
Cue 25	**Dickon:** ". . . see it—or hear it!" *Recording of "Comfort Ye . . ."; music fades and TV news replaces*	(Page 26)

SCENE 7

Cue 26	As CURTAIN rises *Motor-cycle arrives and stops*	(Page 26)
Cue 27	**Blitz** exits, **Lindsey** picks up letter **Millicent's** *recorded voice (optional)*	(Page 29)
Cue 28	**Lindsey** picks up pen and writes **Lindsey's** *recorded voice (optional)*	(Page 29)

SCENE 8

Cue 29	Before CURTAIN rises *Recording of "The Holly and the Ivy"*	(Page 29)

ACT II

SCENE 1

Cue 30	As CURTAIN rises, **Lindsey** reads letter **Lindsey's** *recorded voice (optional)*	(Page 32)
Cue 31	**Lindsey:** ". . . about the new book . . ." *Motor-cycle arrives and stops*	(Page 32)
Cue 32	**Dickon:** ". . . here. In the cottage—" *Car arrives and stops*	(Page 33)
Cue 33	**Lindsey:** ". . . plan the menu . . ." *Door bangs off*	(Page 33)
Cue 34	**Lindsey:** ". . . certainly use them!" **Dickon** *sings to guitar*	(Page 34)

Cue 35	**Voices singing:** ". . . want to earn some bread" *Car starts, revs and drives away*	(Page 34)

SCENE 2

Cue 36	As Scene opens *Guitar plays*	(Page 35)
Cue 37	**Old Ladies** exit *Guitar increases in volume—applause—continue until* **Dickon** *speaks*	(Page 36)
Cue 38	**Chris** enters *Guitar chords and song*	(Page 37)
Cue 39	At end of Scene *Moving car effect (optional)*	(Page 38)
Cue 40	As Scene closes *Car revs up, then fades (optional)*	(Page 38)

SCENE 3

Cue 41	**Lindsey** and **Bellamy** exit *Pause, then car starts up and drives away*	(Page 43)
Cue 42	**Chris:** "Dickon—wait! Come back!" *Motor-cycle revs up and drives away*	(Page 44)

SCENE 4

Cue 43	CURTAIN falls on Scene 3. Slight pause *Telephone rings. Recorded conversation with* **Dr Porteus** *(optional)*	(Page 44)
Cue 44	At start of Scene 4 *Telephone rings*	(Page 45)
Cue 45	**Sister:** ". . . to the dispensary. They'll know . . ." *Ambulance bell as ambulance arrives and stops*	(Page 47)

SCENE 5

Cue 46	**Di** switches on kettle *Pause, then car arrives and stops*	(Page 50)
Cue 47	**Chris:** "Any time." *Car starts up and drives off*	(Page 50)
Cue 48	**Di** runs out with **Blitz** and **Chris** *Sound of smashing glass*	(Page 52)

SCENE 6

Cue 49	**Mrs Bevil:** ". . . see if some could be stuck." *Car starts up and drives off*	(Page 56)

SCENE 7

Cue 50	**Lindsey** starts to read letter **Millicent's** *recorded voice (optional)*	(Page 59)
Cue 51	**Lindsey:** ". . . prefer the Kremlin." *Motor-cycle arrives and stops*	(Page 59)

Effects Plot

Cue 52	**Lindsey** starts to read letter **Dickon's** *recorded voice (optional)*	(Page 61)
Cue 53	**Student:** "... have found peace in this place." *Pause, then motor-cycle starts and revs*	(Page 61)
Cue 54	**Lindsey:** "Just a moment..." *Motor-cycle stops*	(Page 61)
Cue 55	As **Lindsey** faces door, waiting *Song: "The Soft September Air" starts—first verse only—fades with fall of final* CURTAIN	(Page 62)

Printed in Great Britain by Butler & Tanner Ltd, Frome and London

www.ingramcontent.com/pod-product-compliance
Ingram Content Group UK Ltd.
Pitfield, Milton Keynes, MK11 3LW, UK
UKHW021844210426
5322IPUK00022B/463